EVERY
MISTAKE
IN THE BOOK

EVERY MIST∆KE IN THE BOOK

A BUSINESS HOW-*NOT*-TO

F. J. LENNON

ReganBooks

An Imprint of HarperCollins*Publishers*

HarperCollins books may be purchased for educational, business, or sales promotional use. For information please write: Special Markets Department, HarperCollins Publishers Inc., 10 East 53rd Street, New York, NY 10022.

FIRST EDITION

Designed by Renato Stanisic

Printed on acid-free paper

Library of Congress Cataloging-in-Publication Data

Lennon, F. J., 1964–
   Every mistake in the book : a business how-not-to / F. J. Lennon.—1st ed.
     p. cm.
   ISBN 0-06-039393-9
    1. Success in business. 2. Business failures. I. Title.

  HF5386 .L563 2001
  650.1—dc21
                                           2001019401

01 02 03 04 05 CG/RRD 10 9 8 7 6 5 4 3 2 1

For Laura

A life spent making mistakes
is not only more honorable but more useful than
a life spent doing nothing.
—George Bernard Shaw

Every young man would do
well to remember that all successful business
stands on the foundation of morality.
—Henry Ward Beecher

I felt it rather easy to portray a 1970s British businessman.
Being bland, rather cruel and incompetent
comes naturally to me.
—John Cleese

Murphy's Law:
1. Nothing is ever as easy as it looks.
2. Everything takes longer than you think.
3. If anything can go wrong, it will.

Contents

INTRODUCTION

To Err Is Human . . .

If Alexander Pope were alive today to evaluate my business career, he'd choose me as the poster boy for his phrase, "To err is human . . ." Maybe that master of dramatic irony would even be inspired to immortalize me in one of his biting poems or essays. My years in business, after all, have been both ironic and dramatic.

When it comes to business, I may very well have made every mistake in the book. And the mistakes I haven't made, I've witnessed others make. I'm not ashamed to tell you how I've screwed up. Have I been frustrated with myself? Definitely. Angry? A little. But I've never been ashamed because I can say that without a doubt, I've always learned more from my failures than from my successes.

I'm writing this book so that others can learn from the errors of my ways. When you think about it, you won't get too far unless you learn from the mistakes of others; there's no way you'll live long enough to make them all yourself.

My very first business decision was probably also my first mistake. In 1985, I cofounded a computer game company from my college dorm room. It happened by accident. I was majoring in Communications, and though I had no idea what I wanted to do with my life, I was certain that whatever it was, business would play no part in it. Then fate intervened. But before I go there, let me take a step back.

I had always been a lazy kid, the kind who didn't want to do anything that required physical movement—the kind I'm terrified of being the father of someday. My grades were lousy; I'm certain now that I was slightly delusional; and my social life consisted of going to the movies, watching television whenever possible, and dreaming of being the first professional baseball player who didn't have to run. Believe me when I tell you I wasn't very good at anything.

But then along came coin-operated arcade games. It started with Pong in the mid-1970s. Before long I realized that it wouldn't take much work to master the latest games at the mall and the bowling alley near my house, and I was hooked. I studied these early coin-op classics, became obsessed with them, even had dreams about them. Soon I found I could skip a day of school and stretch the three quarters in my pocket into a full day of fun playing Asteroids, Phoenix, Pac-Man, Missile Command, Galaxian, and Donkey Kong. My arcade phase kept me busy until I was seventeen.

Then came college, where I finally hit my stride. For the first time in my life I was brimming with confidence. The arcade seemed like a lifetime ago. Then, during my senior year, something happened that brought the old days back: The martial arts changed my life. No, it wasn't karate lessons—that would have involved getting off the couch. What happened was that I got hooked on a new coin-op game, Karate Champ, and suddenly I was back at it with a vengeance. A few friends and I spent hours learning the game inside out, mastering our kicks and chops on the machine in a pizza shop.

And within a year, we decided to turn our passion into a business with a little money we raised; we started a company that created games for the brand-new IBM PC. The first game, naturally, was a martial arts extravaganza that made little impact in the marketplace. If we had spent as much time making our game as we did playing Karate Champ, we may have had a hit on our hands.

Success didn't come fast. In fact, it barely came at all. During my first year in business, I made the mistake of trusting several consultants, sales reps, and vendors who took advantage of my inexperience and helped themselves to much of my precious seed capital. To me they both looked like solid, well-established business pros; to them, I must have looked like Bambi right after his mother got shot.

Over the next seven years I struggled to keep the business alive in an industry that was changing around me every day. Leo Tolstoy once said, "From the child of five to myself is but a step. But from the newborn baby to the child of five is an appalling distance." The entertainment software industry, in its infancy when I began, journeyed quite an appalling distance during those early years, and I was along for the terrible twos.

As technology advanced from tape-driven computers to the modern PC, and as computer games evolved from text adventures to today's ultraviolent 3-D action games, I did more than fight to keep my company on the cusp of technology. I battled simply to keep my business alive.

During those early years, I wore a lot of hats within the organization. I conceptualized and designed a number of the games. But the creative aspect, always my favorite part of the job, was only a small part of my new life. While I was writing dialogue for elves in role-playing adventures and sketching space aliens on bar napkins, I was also sweating bullets trying to make payroll, raise working capital, fight off lawsuits, battle the IRS, and keep other companies from luring my employees away.

Did I end up on the cover of *Forbes* or *Fortune*? Not even close. But I got an education that I never could have received in a classroom. During those years, one of the few smart things I did was to keep a series of journals. I wrote in them obsessively. One journal was devoted strictly to business mistakes. Needless to say, as competition intensified and our corporate debts grew like a malignant tumor, my mistakes journal got thicker by the day.

Then, in 1992, a miracle occurred. My fledgling business was purchased. Though the company truly had little of value to sell, a large company in our industry that had just gone public was in frantic acquisition mode. When the deal was closed I felt as if I'd just stolen the Hope Diamond: I had a two-year contract and stock options in a public company. I didn't make any significant cash in the sale, but the corporate debts, for which I was responsible, were erased. I had squirmed off the hook and received a miraculous stay of execution. But that wasn't the end of the story—or the mistakes.

I tried to settle into my new job, but I sensed trouble from the start. The company, overaggressive in its expansion, attempted to diversify into new areas without a solid plan. Within months, the entire organization was hemorrhaging cash. Epic screw-ups were occurring by the day, and I knew it was only a matter of time before I'd become an unemployment statistic. That rusty old hook was poised in front of me again. Despite an inner voice that screamed, "Don't do it!" I took a risk. I bought the company back, helped reform it into a new organization, and sold it quickly to another anxious buyer hot to get into multimedia.

I coasted from boondoggle to boondoggle during this period,

and I recorded them all in my journal. My writing became a daily therapeutic exercise. Maybe it was my Catholic upbringing, but recording our daily foul-ups felt like confession—except that there was never absolution, only frustrated investors, furious creditors, and disgruntled employees.

What was supposed to be the birth of a wonderful new company soon became a horror story. I now found myself working for a boy—not an immature man or a short guy prone to tantrums, but literally a guy who was barely old enough to drink a beer, a whelp playing office with his trust fund. Worst of all, he was a sinister little manipulator, a true Machiavelli of multimedia. It didn't take long for tensions to erupt. As this man-child played business tycoon, I found it impossible to mask my disgust. I had no intention of climbing the ladder of success wrong by wrong. I was faced with the same dilemma as Luke Skywalker—either join the dark side or fight it. I decided to fight. Soon I was living in his doghouse, while many others around me were happily residing in his ass.

During the two years I worked in that asylum, I did my best to produce a few decent products and manage my staff fairly—despite corporate politics that played out with all the drama of a Shakespearean tragedy. The whole saga ended badly, and I should have walked away much earlier than I did. During those dark days, I killed quite a few trees fattening my business-mistakes journal.

The year 1996 marked a turning point. When my contract expired I resigned, left the small town where I had grown up and worked, and moved to Los Angeles to pursue a career as a freelancer. As a consultant, I watched as phenomenal mistakes were made by some of the largest companies in the entertainment industry. Again and again, they made my own youthful business indiscretions look as trivial as spilling paint on the floor of my kindergarten class.

I began to relish the freedom that freelancing afforded me. One step removed from the political battlefield, I did my work, took my money, and moved on to the next client, where I could expand my mistakes journal by observing an entirely new cast of characters at work.

After a sixteen-year journey, I had the urge to sift through my journals, present my observations, and compile remedies to my mistakes.

Some of the stories you'll read in this book are pathetic; others are sad; plenty are silly. But all are true. I've changed the names to protect myself from the guilty, but I think I've captured the essence of several unique personalities I've had the misfortune of working with. A few of them may even seem quite familiar to you. I'm sure you'll be able to spot some of their traits among your own coworkers and associates.

The information conveyed in these pages can help anyone involved in business, from those contemplating a dot-com start-up to frustrated managers to disillusioned employees drowning in the filthy cesspool of office politics.

"Someday you'll look back on this and laugh": It's one of the most common consolations in the annals of human behavior. For me, it's an adage that's proven indispensable. Go ahead and laugh at some of the magnificent blunders I'll share with you. And likewise, don't take your own screw-ups too seriously. The mistakes detailed in this book seemed so tragic when I committed them that they drove me into therapy, and fostered a wide array of physical ailments and mental anguish along the way. But despite it all I'm alive and well—and successful—today.

We all make mistakes. That's the beauty of the whole damn story. If the business world could only learn from its mistakes instead of continually repeating them, what a bright future we'd all share.

1

BIZ BASICS

Beware of undertaking too much at the start.
Be content with quite a little. Allow for accidents.
Allow for human nature, especially your own.
—Arnold Bennet

When I started out in business, I didn't have a clue. I'd never even taken a basic finance or marketing course in college. But suddenly I found myself at the helm of a business, and I took a lot of lumps for my inexperience. This section will be especially useful for those contemplating a start-up, but anyone who owns a business already can also benefit from this material. Here are some of the business fundamentals I learned the hard way.

1. ABOVE ALL ELSE, DON'T MAKE CRAP

If you're in business or are contemplating a start-up, this is where to start: *Produce a great product.* If what you're marketing—or the service you're providing—isn't high-quality, you can't succeed. Sounds simple, huh? Well, it's not; it requires a rare combination of innovative ideas, good people, abundant financing—and hard work.

All great products start with a clever idea. Is yours good enough?

Original enough? Would you buy the product you have in mind? Be honest—would you really?

All right, maybe your idea is great. Now you need the most important ingredient of all—cash. Without proper financing, you can have the greatest idea in the world, but still get nowhere. For more on this, see chapter 2, "Money Matters." Money in the bank is what you'll need to hire good people: Talented employees are always expensive, but they're worth every cent.

Once you're on your way, there's a typical start-up Catch-22 you should do your best to avoid. You may find yourself saying, "I'll begin by getting an average product out there, earn a few quick bucks, and *then* get to work on that really great product." Yeah, and Donald Trump is going to start paying his bills on time. If your first product isn't great, chances are slim that you'll ever get started on that second one. *Never bank on tomorrow's product to pull you out of today's mistakes.*

If your company is barely surviving on mediocrity, don't prolong the inevitable. As hard and frightening as it is to do, shoot your business like a gimpy racehorse. *Never borrow money to keep a fledgling operation alive.*

During my initial years in business, I was operating on seed money raised from local doctors, family members, lawyers, and businessmen. Looking back, it was ludicrous to think that I could compete on a national and international level without substantial venture capital. Piecemeal funding led to shoestring product budgets, which in turn made it impossible for my company to produce A-level titles that could compete in the industry. Instead, our C+/B products usually sold just enough copies to keep our doors open.

The fear and uncertainty of failure motivated me to crawl forward. I know now that I should have walked away; I would have been better off closing the operation down and joining a large, well-financed, solidly established company in the industry. If I'd gotten in on the ground floor of a company like Electronic Arts (and I had that opportunity), I could have retired by the time I was thirty. Instead I clung to the dream of owning my own business—but inadequate funding and inexperience made that an impossible dream. Don't make the same mistake.

2. REALLY DOUBLE-CHECK THAT IT'S NOT CRAP

You must take the time to assure the quality of your product. Quality assurance is a hot topic in today's business world. Many companies in my industry are releasing products before they are finished. Why? If the company is public, a late product release might spell collapse for its stock price. If it's privately held, being late with a big-money product launch could mean a serious cash-flow crisis.

But the short-term benefit of selling a lousy, unfinished product pales in comparison to the long-term damage that comes from disappointing or deceiving your customers. Before you consider launching a substandard product, ignore the gun at your head and weigh the consequences honestly. How badly will the public react? I assure you, worse than you can imagine. And they won't forget. *Quality service must be a cornerstone of your business.*

Even minor bugs can ruin a gaming experience, but with all of the variables involved, it's next to impossible to ship a perfectly clean game. That's just the nature of software.

But I've worked for two different companies that ripped off their customers by releasing computer games before they were completed. In both instances, it wasn't just that there were a few bugs to be worked out in a final round of tests. These companies released products that were missing *entire segments* from their original designs. One firm had to meet quarterly numbers to avoid a downgrade in its stock; the other had a public offering in the works. The CEO of this business decided to release a product that was— and I'm not kidding—90 percent incomplete just to get the initial sell-in numbers on the books.

In both cases, the reputations of these companies took a public beating. Industry magazines dubbed them publishers of unfinished vaporware (software that is promised but never actually completed), making them laughingstocks, and irate customers posted raging messages on bulletin boards and chat rooms all over the net.

Of course, this was the world of software, where expectations are often underfulfilled, and somehow these companies managed to survive. But it's not always that easy. Imagine buying a car that went belly-up in a week. Many of today's emerging industries are doing the equivalent, but the public won't put up with poor performance forever.

If you want to succeed in business, have the guts to treat your customers fairly. Give them a product that's worthy of its price tag. Don't let your company be one of the losers that can't see beyond the fine print of the *Wall Street Journal*.

3. YOUR CUSTOMERS AREN'T MORONS

Have respect for your customers. Go to trade shows and soak up opinions, criticism, and comments. Set up surveys to learn what people want and expect. Read E-mail and *respond* to your audience. And spend a day in your customer service department. Not only will you learn a lot about your products, but you'll come to appreciate what a hard job a good customer support representative has. It's not easy to listen to complaints all day. If you don't believe me, take some of those complaint calls yourself. You'll be amazed at what you learn.

Welcome customer feedback. Using questionnaires, E-mail, and research groups, start listening to what the public thinks about your company and its products.

In my experience, the customer isn't always right—just 90 percent of the time. And the truth is, anyone who has contributed a dime to your company's bottom line deserves your respect. Now, I'm not condoning the abuse that's often heaped upon customer support reps. There's a certain percentage of idiots out there who get their rocks off by belittling people over the phone, and every so often one of them will go right to the top with their thundering rage. Don't let them get under your skin. Calm down, watch your tongue, and realize that most people aren't idiots. They just want to be heard.

I can't tell you how many times I've listened to customer support representatives make fun of people who are calling for help. This used to be a common occurrence in my own business. The head of my customer service department would rank the biggest idiots of the month on a bulletin board in his office. One of his winners thought that a CD-ROM was a hard disk, because it was literally a *hard disk*. Another winner was the person who, after being instructed to insert a CD-ROM into his computer, claimed not to know where the drive was. "It'll slide out when you press the little button," the support rep informed him. "The tray is flat so you can lay the disk on it."

"You mean the cup holder?" the caller asked.

It's impossible not to snicker at that story. Hell, I laughed out loud. But I should never have allowed anyone in the company to think for a moment that we didn't need that poor guy on the other end of the phone. At the time I let my customer support manager's attitude slide, mainly because I was worried about issues I considered far more important than a few employees having a laugh or two at the customer's expense. But in retrospect, I should have never tolerated that attitude. It set a bad precedent, and promoted the idea that the people in the company mattered more than the customer. I didn't recognize or respect one of the basic fundamentals of business: without customers, even the obnoxious and stupid ones, there is no business.

4. DON'T GET FAT TOO FAST—YOU'LL NEVER LOSE THE WEIGHT

Stay lean and grow small. Ego-driven growth kills companies. When I started out, my idea of a successful business was a company with a gorgeous office and lots of employees. Hey, that's what J. R. Ewing had on *Dallas*, and it served him well (until he got shot, anyway). Bottom-line numbers didn't figure into my delusions of grandeur. Numbers were for bean counters; I was an entrepreneur.

When my friends and I founded our company, we set up shop in a small apartment. We should have stayed there for years, but what did we do? Within four months we'd leased office space and started hiring employees. Was our first employee a programmer or an artist? No way. Employee number one was a receptionist.

Then it came time to furnish the office. Who got the bigger office, larger desk, and higher-backed chair became critical issues of debate. Somehow, a well-furnished office with people walking around was comforting. If we looked like a real business, how could we ever go out of business?

This senseless need for hollow growth is as old as time; as long as human beings have egos, this whopper of a mistake will keep being made. There are other prime examples of this same mistake in my own industry today. One computer game company had a custom-designed multimillion-dollar office suite constructed atop a skyscraper in a major Southern city, yet as I write this, this band of egocentric misfits hasn't shipped a decent product in their four-year history. They're more concerned with having their pictures in national magazines and having more employees than their rivals down the street than sitting their asses down in their thousand-dollar ergonomic chairs and completing what they started.

If you're building a business from scratch, you're going to have to work very hard, especially in the early days of your business. *Wear many hats in your organization.* Type your own letters. Answer your own phone. Build that bank account even if you have to work around the clock for a year or two. When it comes time to increase your staff, make sure you can carry the weight. When you're hiring someone, look him or her in the eye and pretend you have to say, "Sorry—I screwed up. I have to fire you now. I hope your kid will still be able to get those braces."

Work on top of each other. Forget about securing more office space until it's impossible to move sideways without it. Be sensible. In twenty years, you won't even remember that expensive desk and chair you have your eye on today.

I think I've finally learned this lesson well. I would work in a closet and do every job myself before I would create overhead to make my company look legitimate.

5. DON'T PICK YOUR WORKSPACE BECAUSE IT HAS A PRETTY VIEW

Select your office location carefully. *Pay a good inspector top dollar to pinpoint any problems the landlord should address before you sign a lease.* It never occurred to me to have a rental property inspected until one near-disaster almost put my business under. Less than a year into our lease the roof in our office started leaking, and ugly water spots began staining the ceiling tiles. Water is to computers what kryptonite is to the Man of Steel, and considering that these computers were my company's only hard assets, water leaks posed a major threat. The landlord assured me that the roof was holding up fine—and, trusting nincompoop that I was, I believed him. A few nights later a thunderstorm tore through the area; most of what remained of the roof blew off completely, and water poured into the office like Niagara Falls. Five of our thirteen computers were destroyed, and we were forced to set up shop in a borrowed apartment until we could get back on our feet. My deadbeat landlord tried to dodge his responsibility. Over the next month, most of the employees worked at home; as you can imagine, productivity was nil until we finally settled back into our office. If I had taken the time and spent a few hundred dollars to have the location inspected before we moved in, I could have written that location off and looked for an office with a solid structure and a roof that wasn't held down with Elmer's glue.

Make sure you have plenty of renter's insurance. And always pay your premiums on time. Never, ever let your insurance bills slide because the second you do, your entire organization is vulnerable.

Finally, *pay for a top-notch security system.* During my first year in business, my office was burglarized. Luckily, the thief went straight for the petty cash box and left the computers alone. A more serious burglar could have cleaned us out.

6. DON'T GET ATTENTION DEFICIT DISORDER

Stay focused! Clear your head, take a deep breath, and ask yourself, "What do I have to do today?" Not tomorrow, or next week, or next month. *Today.*

It's easy to lose focus on the present when you're worrying about the future. But realize this: You can't reach a destination without taking the specific daily steps that will ultimately lead you there. To succeed in business, you have to train your mind to take a far-off vision, bring it into focus, and break it into minute details. Then you must take these minute details and organize them into daily tasks. All that's required then is the courage to commit to the completion of these daily tasks—despite the obstacles in your way—with utter faith that your original vision will be brought to life.

Fear is the enemy. At least it's mine. In the times in my life when I've been floundering, it's been fear that kept me from following up on important day-to-day tasks. You may hear those troubling inner voices whispering, "What if this doesn't work? What if I'm wrong?"; self-doubt is natural. But you have to rise just far enough above that doubt to keep working or you're doomed. The best way I've found to get past my fear is to forget it. And to forget it, I need to get lost in a project. Throw yourself so far into your work that you keep the fear at a reasonable distance. If you do that well enough, the fear won't cripple you, at least not until your daily work is done.

Create realistic, manageable schedules, and always be on top of your next milestone. Once you start to let important deadlines slip, you're digging your grave. Falling behind after you've created a logical, realistic plan is a cardinal sin. Keep all of your employees focused on their goals, too. Many employees I've managed have been unfocused, especially the highly creative ones. They spend their time trying to do next month's job, and forget about today's. You have to teach some people to walk one step at a time. Be patient. Sometimes you'll feel like a baby-sitter, but it's critical if you're going to keep your project on track. All it takes is one weak link, and you'll lose control of the whole development process.

It's also easy to lose complete focus when you're attempting to diversify into new areas. *Never be stupid enough to branch out in multiple directions until you've perfected your core business.* That was the big mistake made by one of the companies in my industry. The CEO of this organization, full of phony bravado and guts, could have starred in a parody sketch about Napolean. Like the fearless warrior he wasn't, His Majesty the Emperor tried to conquer the coin-operated game world on top of his core business, PC games. Coin-op games and computer games may sound like the same thing, but they're completely different businesses. Coin-op games are extremely expensive to produce, they're always fast-paced and action-oriented, and the audience (mostly young boys) either loves 'em or hates 'em. It's a hit-or-miss business, with no middle ground. Either your game machine is full of quarters at the end of the night, or it's the dusty one in the back with the Slurpee puddle on the control panel. Worst of all, in some cases, the distribution network for coin-op machines can be controlled by some pretty unsavory characters. The Emperor and his lackeys never took the time to investigate the basics before plunging into the coin-op world, so the company's venture flopped and began a downward spiral that all but destroyed the entire organization.

I've found it hard to maintain focus when I've been forced to work with manic personalities. These aren't stupid people, just erratic and insecure—bundles of temperamental nervous energy. You know the type—the kind of person who starts a thousand little projects on Monday morning, but by Tuesday is overwhelmed, by Wednesday bored, by Thursday disillusioned, and by Friday, ready to escape. This kind of person often has all kinds of crazy notions that serve no purpose but to knock an entire project off track. I do my best to ignore these personality types until their distracting notions pass, but that often takes weeks—weeks we all could and should be focusing 100 percent on what we've set out to do in the first place.

7. DON'T FALL ASLEEP AT YOUR STATION

Early in my career, I didn't analyze what my competitors were up to. I seldom relied on market research to suggest the kinds of products that I should be developing. We would just think up a new idea for a game and start making it. Needless to say, we never saw changing consumer trends coming early enough; often, by the time we'd completed a new product, its audience had vanished.

Don't just learn the tricks of your trade. *Learn your trade.* You have to know your industry from top to bottom. That means keeping up on new consumer trends, as well as knowing what each of your competitors is up to.

Subscribe to every one of your industry's trade magazines. Surf the web for interesting sites that will help keep you up to date on new technologies and innovations. One good eight-hour day surfing the Internet should help you discover any number of relevant web sites that you can bookmark and revisit weekly. Most, if not all, of the companies in your industry will have corporate web sites. Revisit them often to stay abreast of what your competitors are up to.

Find a source for quality market research. This information can be expensive, but solid consumer data and accurate industry sales figures will send alarm bells clanging if you're producing out-of-date products no one will want.

Consumer trends have changed continuously in my own industry. When I started in 1985, text games were the craze; there was no need for animation. Time to hire those writers. Then along came graphic adventure games, and they were the rage. Time to hire those artists. About the time adventure games began to die, a few years later, role-playing games became the hot property. Time to hire those *Dungeons and Dragons* geeks. A couple of years after that, role-playing began to falter, and graphic adventures reemerged along with strategy games. Now role-playing has made a comeback, but bloody first-person 3-D kill-everything-in-sight action shooters dominate the market. Time to hire those ex-cons.

If I'd paid more attention to shifting trends when I started, I could have adjusted my product plans, saved a fortune, and started producing products that had a chance to hit the charts. Instead, a few of my products were hailed by research experts as proof positive that the genres we were serving were dead indeed.

Like all living matter, a business must evolve to survive, and industry knowledge greatly aids the evolutionary process. If you know your business and your audience, you can anticipate market changes early, adjust accordingly, and survive.

8. KNOW WHERE THE BIG BUCKS ARE

You're in business to make money. And to do that, *you've got to know what it takes to reach the mass market, where the big dollars flow.* You can start to feel the pulse of the marketplace if you learn to listen to your gut feelings and use your brain. Open your eyes to popular trends. Become aware of the world around you. Some people are born with an instinct for tracking business trends, but even an amateur can learn to keep an ear to the ground.

In my own industry, I now study not only the computer game industry, but the entertainment business in general. I see all of the top-grossing movies. I know what television shows are most popular. I watch MTV. I pay attention to what toys children play with. I visit toy stores and keep abreast of the comic book industry. I visit a bookstore at least once a week, and browse the bestseller lists and industry magazines every Sunday.

It takes time to get to know your market, but it's time well spent. And don't be an intellectual snob about it. I can't stand it when people in the entertainment industry boast that they never watch television. How can you understand what drives Americans to buy unless you study the content on that box that does most of the driving?

Knowing what's hot is only half the equation. Understanding *why it's hot* is just as important. What is Eminem's appeal? Why are wrestling ratings and pay-per-view revenues skyrocketing? Why is everyone glued to their televisions watching prime-time trivia game shows or reality TV? Ask yourself these kinds of questions, and draw your own conclusions. Dig deep. Search. The answers will come.

Sometimes the answers won't be obvious. I can't explain why *The Waterboy* was one of the top-grossing films of 1998. Nor can I fully comprehend why the public is so fixated on watching steroid freaks pound each other over the head with chairs several nights a week on cable television. Yet wrestling is a cultural phenomenon that is grossing a bloody fortune. And understanding—or at least recognizing—this trend might help explain why today, in my industry, "shoot-em-up" games are the rage. Whether or not I myself enjoy wrestling or love action pictures or would stand in line in the rain to buy a Britney Spears concert ticket is of no importance. What's important is that I'm aware of these consumer trends.

Don't let your tastes alone dictate your product decisions. Let the public speak . . . and *listen*.

9. YOU BETTER HAVE A GIMMICK

Do something unique so that people recognize your product or company. Make your packaging, advertising, and promotional items stand out. Try something that no competitor has thought to do. Make your presence known. It's not as hard as it seems. There's not a lot of originality out there.

Look at the phenomenal success of the marketing campaign for the movie *The Blair Witch Project*. The promoters of that film knew that the originality of their marketing material was going to have to be more important than what that material cost. No one in the entertainment industry had, to that point, brought the Internet, film, television, and word of mouth together to market a film in such an intriguing way. And because they had the ingenuity to do something totally fresh, they are now some of the most sought-after marketers in the entertainment business.

Innovative marketing has also been rewarded in my own industry. In the late 1980s, a game company called Psygnosis had what I still consider to be the best packaging in the business. Unlike the busy-looking game packages by everyone else in the industry, their titles were packaged in glossy jet-black boxes with cover art by Roger Dean, the artist who painted the Yes album covers. I knew immediately when I saw one of those cool black boxes that I was looking at a Psygnosis game.

The boxes for Infocom text adventures always came with little gimmick items that served as clues for the mystery—scraps of paper with notes scrawled on them, business cards with addresses, even takeout restaurant menus. These little clues were irresistible, and what made them cooler was that they didn't cost the company a fortune. I used to look forward to the toys in the box more than the game itself, and I'm sure there were plenty of avid buyers who felt the same way.

In the animation-driven games business, my company was the first to show real people in our print advertisements. Most of the ads in the industry featured cartoon artwork taken directly from the games, but we set out to do something totally different. For our first game we hired an Asian black belt, who wore an authentic ninja hood. We used a close-up of his eyes for our ad campaign. For another game, in which a player was charged with rescuing his kidnapped girlfriend, we hired professional models and shot a bunch of moody film noir photos in an abandoned warehouse. We turned them into a stylish ad, and soon we found that our efforts were getting noticed. These ads helped put my company on the map.

So how did I go wrong in this department? I guess my big mistake was that I was spending heavy advertising dollars on mediocre products. I never had trouble coming up with cool ad gimmicks. My problem was paying for them.

Which provides a great segue to my next topic . . .

10. DON'T WASTE YOUR MONEY MARKETING CRAP

Avoid overaggressive marketing for mediocre products. I've made the mistake of sinking a fortune into marketing and advertising campaigns for products that didn't stand a chance of becoming a hit. How could I do something that stupid? I think the problem may have been denial. Even with small production budgets, we tried like hell to make products that could compete with the big boys. I suppose I felt that if I didn't advertise the products, I would be giving up on them, and that was impossible for me to do after I'd expended so much energy creating them. So, regardless of how good or bad a product was, I sank serious capital into packaging, advertising, and promotional materials—money that should have gone into development.

Don't make that mistake. Be honest with yourself. Is your product great? Can it compete? If you have even an inkling of doubt, don't spend money creating and placing ads or expensive sales materials. You might as well start a campfire and shovel your cash into the flames. Get your product to the market, try to recoup your development costs, do some good old-fashioned PR work (which doesn't cost as much), and invest what you would have spent marketing an inferior product in creating a better one.

11. MAKE MONEY, THEN ART

Dream in a pragmatic way.
—Aldous Huxley

A creative executive for one of the world's top interactive entertainment companies I worked for once told me, "We're here to make art." He actually showed disdain for products that were delivered on time and under budget. Needless to say, after his division hemor-rhaged money for nearly eighteen months, this executive—whom I'll call Lenny DaVinci—was fired along with the rest of the top-tier management staff, and replaced with serious bean counters. The last thing Lenny told me before being escorted out of the building was, "It's for the best. How could I work for a company that only cares about making a profit?"

I wish Lenny well on whatever planet he now inhabits. Here on earth, businesses *must* make a profit. That's the whole point of the game.

I believe the greatest achievement of any entrepreneurial venture is the creation of jobs. Employing human beings is the noblest thing a company does. But without profits, no new jobs are created. In fact, existing jobs are cut—and it's jokers like Lenny who are often to blame.

I know for a fact that one of the biggest names in computer game design is actually an overrated no-talent who screwed over his fellow employees because he started to believe the media stories portraying him as a brilliant digital *artiste*. He's the Yoda of the biz, the (so-called) designer of one of the best-selling and top-rated games ever. Truth be known, he ripped off most of his ideas from old board games. He was even sued by the creator of one of these notable games, but the case was settled quickly. Yoda also relied heavily on smarter, younger, and more talented people who were thrilled by his very presence—and willing to let him take credit.

After Yoda topped the charts with his megahit, his eagerly antici-pated follow-up went into production. But halfway through devel-opment, Yoda lost his inspiration and gave up—right about the time that hundreds of thousands of orders were being placed for the game. Without an existing idea to lift, Yoda was lost, and because "his creative heart just wasn't in it," the company lost millions and several dozen employees were let go. While the innocent victims marched to the unemployment office, Yoda maintained his exorbitant salary—and began scanning the globe for another obscure idea to steal.

One of the biggest flaws of people like Lenny and Yoda is that they have no clue what is possible and what is impossible in relation to their projects. *Don't lose track of the real world.* I appreciate creative work as much as anyone, but creative brainstorming without a budget or a concrete design is a waste of time.

A few years ago, I spent a few days brainstorming with a group that was the so-called "creative heart and soul" of one of the true entertainment powerhouses. I was excited to sit in, at long last, on one of the high-energy sessions I'd heard about for years. What I ended up attending was an unfocused free-for-all, in which a room full of carnival barkers spewed out all sorts of fantastic notions, every one of them completely impossible in the context of the project we were discussing. It became a sad kind of pissing match, in which each new person, anxious to outdo the last impossible dreamer, shouted out an even more grandiose notion. It was like sitting in a room with a bunch of peacocks, all trying to spread their feathers at once.

For two days I watched these peacocks strut. At first I was frustrated; then I just let myself laugh at the frivolity of it all. Whenever I tried to rein in the discussion by pointing out that the ideas being proposed wouldn't be technologically possible for at least a hundred years, they all just looked at me as if I was a party pooper.

For me, it was a complete waste of time. For the company, *it was a waste of time and money.* I guess I shouldn't complain; the catered lunches were spectacular. Those buffets probably cost more than some of my early product budgets. Hollywood can be a great place to eat. But imagine being the poor sucker upstairs who had to pay for all that verbal masturbation—with nary a plausible idea to show for it.

12. DON'T PUT OLD SHIT IN A SHINY NEW BOX

Here's a common scenario I've witnessed after years of struggling: A company finally creates a hit product. Does that company take a step back and invest some of the financial benefits of that hit to help them expand intelligently upon their successful franchise? No way. Most companies in this position rape their successful projects by releasing the same product over and over again in a series of flimsy disguises.

A company with a hit product should proceed with caution and cherish their franchise like a newborn. I still dream of being in this position. I would take the time to develop a hit product into the cornerstone of my business, not sacrifice it as a short-term cash cow. I would make sure that each new offering took the original product a step or two farther. Not a hundred steps at once, just a slow, steady progression forward.

In my industry, Electronic Arts is a company that respects its prized franchise, EA Sports. Their games are consistently good. But one of their competitors met a sadder fate this year. This company had several successful flight combat franchises, but they destroyed them by releasing mediocre variations on the same old product. Soon enough, customers learned not to come back.

13. GIVE PEOPLE WHAT THEY WANT, NOT WHAT YOU THINK THEY SHOULD HAVE

Never create products to please yourself. Make what the marketplace is screaming for. I've made this critical mistake more than once. In 1987, I wasted a lot of time developing a text adventure game about going back in time to save President Kennedy. Despite the fact that text adventure was quickly going the way of the Edsel, I kept the project alive. Why did I do such a stupid thing? Because I wanted to finish that game—for myself.

That product should have been cancelled the minute I recognized that the marketplace had changed, but I pushed on and released it, and my mistake led to a cash-flow crisis that was nearly impossible to survive. At the time, a respectable-selling game sold 30,000 copies. My product died an even crueler death than JFK; it didn't even crack the thousand-copy mark. It wasn't a total loss—those big old floppy disks we failed to sell made great coasters—but it was a serious body blow.

When I decided to become a freelancer in 1996, I had a hard time remembering this lesson. For eleven years, I'd been accustomed to controlling my own products. As a freelancer, though, I had to learn how give my clients what they wanted, not what I wanted to give them—a tough pill to swallow indeed. Imagine taking Woody Allen, known for exacting total control over his work, and forcing him to appease a totem pole full of movie executives eager to leave their marks on his project. Woody's glasses would melt. For a solid year, that's how I felt.

Several movies in recent years have spoofed the Hollywood creative process. If you've ever watched *The Player, Swimming with Sharks,* or *The Big Picture* and wondered if these movies resembled the truth, I assure you that they do. After five years in L.A., I still haven't been able to distinguish the fine line between parody and reality.

It's hard enough listening to ludicrous ideas, but to actually have to develop them was maddening. Lenny DaVinci, our friend with the art-for-art's-sake tattoo, was a buzzword addict. He wanted computer games to be "immersive," "elegant," and "robust." As opposed to what? Non-robust? Just scan the quotes in *Variety* on any given day and you'll see what the hot buzzwords are. Pretty soon, you'll be hearing them in your own office. Even if you're in the heartland, Hollywood buzzwords will find their way to you as long as there's a Lenny in your life (and I know there is).

Then there was Bobby Fischer, an executive producer who wanted me to incorporate a chess game into a software product for five-year-olds. When I ventured the opinion that checkers would be more appropriate for the age group, Bobby protested, explaining that he was already playing chess by the time he was five. Yeah, right. If he was playing chess at five, I guess his mental powers had already crested and begun to ebb before he learned the Hokey Pokey. Luckily I ended up winning that debate, or there would have been several preschoolers having nap time in front of their computers.

But sadly, I don't win all of my arguments. In fact, I hardly win any. Why? Because of the law of the jungle that says:

"He who payeth, haveth the sayeth."

If you want to keep working, you can't start thinking the world arises in the morning awaiting instructions from you. I've learned to distance myself emotionally from a lot of my contract work in a way I never could when I was in control of a project from beginning to end. I'm a hired gun, and if someone is paying me, I do what they tell me to do, count the days until my contract expires, and move on.

Don't curse my name just yet; I'm not a total sellout. I always have a few projects in the works that I have creative control over. That's how I stay sane.

14. DON'T TRY TO WIN THE INDY 500 IN A MODEL T

To remain competitive in any industry, you must have state-of-the-art technology on your side. If the competition is better equipped, they carry a big advantage into the marketplace.

This was one of my biggest obstacles I faced when I owned my own business. While the industry leaders were developing graphics and special visual effects on Silicon Graphics workstations, all I could afford were archaic IBM clones with 386 processors. It took five of my artists two days to produce something that one artist could crank out in an hour with state-of-the-art hardware and software.

Don't fool yourself into believing that you can win a showdown if your opponent has a gun and you're holding a baseball bat. You need the best technology your industry offers if you want to be tops in your industry. Maybe leading the field is not your goal. There are plenty of companies that turn healthy profits by staying a lap behind the technological leaders. If that's your aim, then press on. But if you want to thrive and not just survive, be equipped.

15. DELIVER THE GOODS

Make sure you can deliver what you promise. Don't oversell yourself, or build hype for products that you can't deliver. I made this mistake often, especially early in my career, and learned my lesson fast. In 1987, by putting on a smoke-and-mirrors corporate pitch that would have made Houdini proud, I was able to convince the biggest publisher in the entertainment software industry to publish my company's products—which were mediocre at best. I flew out to visit the publisher instead of having them fly in to visit my fledgling operation. I stayed in an expensive hotel in San Francisco to bolster the illusion that I was solidly financed. I bought dinner and drinks. I talked up my investors, and boasted about the cutting-edge "artificial intelligence" (the hottest buzzword that year) that made our products light-years ahead of the competition's. I said whatever I had to, true or untrue, to land that deal.

It worked, but less than a year after the deal was signed, my contract with the publisher was terminated. There was no way I could ever deliver what I'd promised, and it didn't take long for my publisher to figure that out.

This kind of overselling happens in every industry, but it especially seems to flourish in emerging industries that have not matured—industries like my own. Just a few years ago, the company I was working for was approached by a completely maniacal game designer who claimed in his twenty-one-page query letter that he was a "genius" and that he had created "the computer game by which all other games in history would be judged." His game, as described, sounded slightly less ambitious than God's creation of the universe. It was (and still remains) the most outrageous letter I've ever read in my career.

Yet this rambling gaming manifesto was not enough to scare away the CEO of our company. Unbelievably, despite a slew of voices advising him against it (mine included), the CEO actually bought into this megalomaniac's delusion and signed a contract to publish his digital opus.

After two years, in which the entire melodramatic soap opera played out in the press, this loose cannon of a game designer fell flat on his face and was swallowed alive by his self-created hype. By then I was long gone, but the company was raked through the coals for releasing an unfinished product, and the designer became the laughingstock of the industry. His name is still bandied about as a synonym for vaporware.

Illusions and BS can only carry you so far. Sooner or later, you have to deliver.

16. KEEP INVESTORS WELL INFORMED

If a group or an individual has enough faith to invest in you, that person or group deserves your courtesy and respect. I may sound like Richie Cunningham, but I really believe it. Your investors should be kept abreast of your progress, or lack of progress, on a consistent, almost daily basis.

When I started out, no venture capital firm would even consider funding my fledgling operation because I was too young and inexperienced. It took funding from local individual investors to get my business off the ground. The piecemeal capital I raised was never enough to build a competitive company, but it was enough to get the business on its feet.

I will always be grateful to the dozen or so investors who believed in me enough to fund our start-up. In many ways, these investors paid for my real education—not a college diploma, but a real education earned through on-the-job experience. I still wonder why these investors did what they did. Maybe they were looking for a tax write-off; perhaps they really believed, as I did at the time, that my company could hit it big. Whatever the case, these brave souls had the faith to part with hard-earned cash so that a group of young people could take a chance and learn, with real consequences at stake. My hat's off to all of them.

Looking back, though, I regret not being more honest with them. When times were good, I'd send out inflated press releases shouting our praises from the mountaintop. But when times were bad—which was most of the time—I'd try to hide it. Why? I hated conflict. And I always believed that what the investors didn't know wouldn't hurt them.

It was a mistake I repeated endlessly in my twenties. During one cash-flow crisis, events spun out of control. We were draining a corporate credit line in an effort to keep our company afloat. None of the investors, including the ones who were personally guaranteeing the credit line, knew what we were doing. It all hit the fan when the manager of the bank called one of our investors to let him know that the credit line was nearly tapped.

This hot-tempered investor showed up at the office like a rabid pit bull looking for a chihuahua to eat. I was on the receiving end of the lambasting of my life, and from that day forward, the investors began exerting tighter control over us.

Honesty, even brutal honesty, is the best policy. It's another squeaky-clean philosophy, but there's no way around it. Don't lie; don't leave any surprises in your bag. Dig deep and muster the courage to be honest, in good times and bad. Don't make excuses. Take responsibility if you're at fault, and if the problem is out of your immediate control, explain why and don't accept the blame.

Always remember what I often forgot: An investment isn't a loan. Loans must be repaid. Investments are speculative—they may or may not pay off. You don't owe your investors money (unless they're loaning the money). But you do owe them two things: your best effort and the truth.

17. ZIP YOUR LIP

It's impossible to say something stupid with your mouth shut. Don't let anyone in business know too much about your private life, your background, or your financial status. That goes for your coworkers as well as outside business associates.

Many a time has my big mouth gotten me into trouble and cost me money. During negotiations, when substantial dollars were at stake, I had a bad habit of giving away the farm without even knowing I was doing it. Time and again, I divulged too much information about my company's finances to the person on the other side of the negotiating table. Why? Because, jackass that I was, I naively believed that everyone—even the person I was bargaining with—was my friend. And weren't friends supposed to share everything? Once my opponent (and that's what the person on the other side of the table usually was) knew everything about me, he stole the advantage.

This lesson really sank in when it came time to sell my company. The buyer refused to propose a deal or name a price until I disclosed everything about my company, including our entire financial history—complete with a breakdown of the amounts that each of our shareholders had invested and loaned. The smart play would have been to share the financial data only after the buyer made an initial offer; terrified that the deal might fall through, though, I handed them everything they wanted on a silver platter. With all of our financials in hand, they now knew exactly how to exploit our vulnerabilities and squeeze us into giving away the company for virtually nothing.

At least when someone tricked me into spilling my guts, I had someone to blame. But when pure ego drove me to say and do stupid things, like bragging and showing off in an attempt to impress business associates, I had no one to blame but myself. If you crow about how rich your company is, if you show off your sportscar, those you're negotiating with may deduce that you don't need all of that money you're negotiating for. People form powerful judgments based on what you say and don't say, do and don't do. Guard your privacy—and don't let anyone on the outside peek into your true inner circle.

It has been difficult for me to tame my tongue, but for the most part I'm now pretty cautious about the information I dole out. When I find myself up against someone who's trying to grill me for information, I remember one mantra: *Be an enigma.* It's nobody's business what makes you or your business tick.

One of my old bosses, a truly miserable little prick, had one of the best poker faces in the business. His eyes were lifeless and gray; he stumbled around in a constant state of grogginess. His flat, monotone voice never varied in pitch or volume; whether he was angry or ecstatic, he sounded like a pager set on vibrator mode. But his zombie-like demeanor made him nearly impossible to read, and his aloofness almost always played to his advantage.

This guy taught me a thousand lessons about how not to behave as a human being, but he also taught me one beneficial lesson: a good poker face is a valuable weapon in your business arsenal.

18. DON'T BE AN UGLY AMERICAN

Respect the customs and cultures of your business associates. If you're going to expand into a foreign country, use locals to help get the operation up and running. Appoint a native of that country to supervise the proceedings, and never be a Damned Yankee.

Shortly after I began working for a guy I'll call Yankee Doodle Dumb-Ass, we made a trip together to Hong Kong to visit a company he had just acquired. I was immediately impressed with the organization and its products.

Alas, within a day, the true purpose of our trip was revealed, and it had nothing to do with employees or products. True to his own horrible nature, Yankee Doodle cared nothing about the talent in the organization. He had his eyes on the company's healthy bank balance, and he planned to liquidate the business so that he could walk away with its cash and assets. Okay, so business isn't always pretty. Sometimes when there's a buck to be made, companies get shut down; I can live with that. But I couldn't live with what he did next.

Without any warning, Yankee Doodle made the president of that organization announce that she was permanently closing the operation, effective immediately. The problem was "immediately" was the day before Chinese New Year, the most celebrated holiday of the year. The president protested, but her objection fell on deaf ears. It was like firing a group of Western workers on Christmas Eve: Yankee Doodle had joined the ranks of Scrooge.

I watched silently as a long parade of shell-shocked employees packed up their belongings and walked out of the building like zombies. One of the company's accountants was deputized to organize all of the financial data by day's end, but rather than stay late and miss a holiday meal with his family, he resigned at five o'clock.

Yankee Doodle scrambled to get another bookkeeper to finish the job, but every member of the financial department declined, and nothing Yankee Doodle said or promised could convince them to stay.

But Yankee Doodle wasn't finished pissing on Chinese custom just yet. There were plenty of other customs left to be violated. On Chinese New Year, it's customary for the employees of an organization to be treated to a company-funded holiday dinner. Likewise, employees receive a double paycheck on the payday preceding the holiday. In most cases, this isn't just a company-funded bonus. Employees actually pay into this fund during the year, much like Americans do when they open Christmas Club accounts. Yankee Doodle thumbed his nose at both of these customs. He cancelled the dinner and withheld the bonus checks.

The guilt-ridden president of the organization dipped into her own pocketbook and paid for the company dinner. My attendance at the dinner didn't win me any points with Yankee Doodle, but I didn't care; it was a memorable event that I shared with fine people. We laughed, talked about software, ate shark fin soup, and drank a lot of beer.

19. DON'T GET NAILED TO THE BOARD

If you've ever been asked to sit on a board of directors—for either the company where you work or another firm—you should feel proud. You're important. You've made a mark. Someone at the top respects you. But before you blindly leap aboard the board, think twice.

Directors of major corporations undoubtedly relish their prestigious positions; they're paid hefty sums for their participation, and enjoy perks like off-site board meetings at world-class resorts. But *with the prestige and perks come hidden risk and responsibility.* Members of corporate boards can be held accountable for the performance of the company, in good times and bad. In some instances, board members can even be held liable for corporate misdeeds of which they themselves may have had no knowledge.

When my own business was facing bankruptcy, several creditors threatened to sue a few of my wealthy board members personally in an attempt to recoup their accounts receivable. Neither I nor most of the directors in my company—the local doctors, lawyers, and businessmen who were investors—had any idea that we could actually be held accountable for the company's bad debts.

When it's time to decide whether to join a board of directors or not, ask yourself this question: Do I really know what's going on inside the company? If you're comfortable with your answer, go for it. When in doubt, respectfully decline.

20. IF YOU'RE GOING TO SUE, DRAW FIRST BLOOD

If you're in business, odds are that sooner or later you're going to be facing a lawsuit. Regardless if you're the suer or the suee, lawsuits are a major pain in the ass. I've been on both sides several times in my career, but there's one mistake I made regarding lawsuits that really stands out.

In 1993, I reached an oral agreement to merge my business with another company. The negotiations went smoothly. A few days after we agreed on terms, this company followed up with an initial draft of the proposed agreement. I reviewed the document carefully and two days later submitted my proposed revisions, but then the company's CEO threw me the mother of all curveballs: He reneged on the agreement, claiming that after a board meeting he could not proceed with the merger. At first I thought it was just a negotiating strategy, but he wasn't kidding; the deal was off. I couldn't understand what went wrong. Just days before, everyone had been gung ho on the deal; we all bolted from the conference room after agreeing on terms and started tossing a football around the parking lot like a bunch of Kennedys at Hyannisport. Now, without warning or a reasonable explanation, the CEO had handed me a ticking time bomb. And the survival of my company was at stake.

Anger overcame me. "I'll sue the bastards," I stammered to everyone within earshot.

With an oral agreement and a draft of the contract in hand, I marched to my lawyer's office. Johnnie Cochran this guy wasn't. He advised me to send the CEO a formal letter informing him that unless the company paid the entire amount laid forth in the contract, I would sue them in ten days. "They'll settle," he assured me.

We sent the letter and waited. The response came two days later in the form of a bogus lawsuit. They were suing me for slander for some insults I hurled at the CEO when he told me the deal was off. Instead of forcing a settlement, I was now forced to countersue the company. Worse, I was forced to countersue them in their own jurisdiction. If and when the case made it to court, it would take place on their home turf. I would have to send my lawyer on the road, or else hire an attorney from that region to represent me. Either way would cost me a fortune, so I had to find a way to squirm out of the lawsuit. The company was quick to offer a solution—they agreed to drop their ridiculous suit if I agreed to drop my legitimate one. With egg all over my face, I gave in.

If I had sued the company immediately, without warning, they would have been forced to defend themselves on my turf—a costly and risky endeavor they'd have been glad to avoid. Chances are, they would have settled, and I would have walked away with a sizable sum. Instead, I slunk off with nothing in my pocket but a bill for two grand in legal fees.

So, the moral of this story is threefold:

1. Hire a good lawyer. Cheaper is not better. Make sure your lawyer didn't graduate from the Benedict Arnold School of Law, or a correspondence course advertised in the back of *Mad* magazine.

2. Don't give your opponent the advantage of striking first. Be like the smart kid in the schoolyard who lands the first punch while the bully is still taking off his jacket. Forget gentlemanly etiquette. Don't tell them what you plan to do, just do it.

3. Make sure you go after not only what you're owed, but your legal fees as well. **Never pay your lawyer; make someone else do it.**

Believe me, I've learned these lessons well. A few years after my merger fiasco, I parted ways with a horrible company. I was to receive a severance package broken into three separate payments. Knowing that the CEO's philosophy was "never pay anyone until they sue you," I prepared myself for the inevitable showdown. I hired a lawyer to do the prep work for the lawsuit weeks before the first check was due. My ever-predictable ex-boss didn't surprise me; he missed the first payment and when I tried to chase him, refused to take my calls. One of his lackeys informed me that the company was having a tough time, and no one was sure when I would be paid.

I hung up the phone, speed-dialed my attorney, and green-lighted the lawsuit. I knew the company was meeting with various underwriters and venture capitalists, so the CEO couldn't afford the trouble I was about to cause. And I was right: within hours his lackey called me to iron out the problem. I told her I would drop my suit only if the company cut me a check for the entire amount they owed me and sent it via overnight express. They did.

21. SHOW THEM THE MONEY

In every area of business, you get what you pay for. This adage is especially true when it comes to employees. They're the lifeblood of your company; don't nickel and dime them to death.

Once your employees have proven themselves, treat them fairly by paying them what they're worth. It's never easy. You'll be paying salaries that seem high, but do it anyway. Spending money to build a top-notch team is an investment, not an expense.

If you can't afford to pay competitive salaries, you shouldn't be hiring. Don't demand or expect talented people to work for peanuts just because you've promised them future glory if and when your ship comes in.

My own business almost always faced cash-flow problems, so I was often forced to hire fresh talent out of local colleges and art schools. My company was like a training ground, with industry new-comers appearing like clockwork to learn their trade and hone their skills before moving on to larger companies where they could earn better wages. It became increasingly difficult to keep talent, and without experienced pros to balance out the newcomers, the quality of our products suffered.

While it's important to pay your employees fairly, though, don't go overboard. *Pay your employees what they are worth and not a cent more.* And never allow yourself to be blackmailed. If an employee threatens to quit unless he gets a raise that isn't justified, let him walk. I learned this lesson a few years ago. I awarded a mediocre employee a raise and promotion that were uncalled for just to prevent her defection because turnover was thought to be too high that quarter. Soon the rest of the employees followed their coworker's lead by threatening to quit unless they received the same treatment. I ended up having to award a number of raises just to keep my people working.

Remember, if you do it for one, you'll inevitably be forced to do it for everyone; don't kiss a prima donna's ass—kick it out the door.

22. PUT A LEASH ON YOUR TALENT

The loss of experienced, talented employees was always devastating to my company. Early in my career, a handful of my employees defected and formed their own company a few miles away and a bitter rivalry ensued. As the competition between our companies intensified, we began raiding each other's organizations. It became an idiotic game of one-upmanship as we tried everything we could to steal bodies from each other. This insidious raiding had everything to do with ego and nothing to do with strengthening our businesses. It didn't matter how talented the employees I was targeting were; as long as they were working for the enemy, I'd hire them in a second.

It was a shameful chess game, and inevitably the real people I treated as pawns were the ones who suffered. When layoffs occurred, the employees that I raided were usually the first ones cut. Some fine people paid the price for my immaturity; of all the business mistakes I've made, this is the one I'm probably most ashamed of.

I took the rivalry to a new level when I instituted a noncompete, nondisclosure policy. All my employees were required to sign a document that prevented them from disclosing any company information or technology to anyone outside the company. Likewise, employees who left the company were prohibited from working for any direct competitor within a 200-mile radius.

No court in the land would uphold such a ridiculously constraining document, but most of the employees didn't know that. Only one of thirty-five employees refused to sign the agreement. Once I instituted that policy, I felt as if I'd won the war. My competitors down the street could no longer raid me, but I could still raid them—at least for another week or two, until they got wind of what I'd done and instituted the same noncompete, nondisclosure policy. The only employee I raided before they got wise was a lummox of an employee who lived at the snack machine and was fired less than a year later for regularly nodding off in front of his computer.

Employee contracts are a more professional way to keep your employees, but contracts are risky. Your company will be forced to live by the provisions of employment contracts, so make sure they are worded carefully.

You should sign your most talented employees to binding contracts—but only after your business has survived its growing pangs and is on solid ground. Even then, protect yourself by having provisions drafted into the agreement that give you leverage. Be fair, but protect yourself first. Some employees feel free to coast after they've managed to secure a contract—and they may be able to get away with it if your contracts leave room for interpretation. Make sure you have clear provisions that allow you to cancel employment contracts for substandard performance, or if your business hits the skids.

Regardless of whether you utilize employment contracts or non-compete agreements, do something to tie your best employees down, or they'll be easy pickings for your competitors.

23. REORGANIZATION WON'T CURE A TERMINAL DISEASE

We trained hard . . . but it seemed that every time we were beginning to form up into teams we would be reorganized. I was to learn later in life that we tend to meet any new situation by reorganizing; and a wonderful method it can be for creating the illusion of progress while producing confusion, inefficiency, and demoralization.
—Petronius Arbiter, 210 B.C.

Progress always means change, but change does not always mean progress.
—Dr. Laurence J. Peter

Reorganization—the dreaded "R" word—has become a truly disturbing trend in today's business culture. Sweeping changes are often necessary within organizations, especially when excellent employees outgrow their jobs, new jobs are added, the company expands, or it falls on hard times. But reorganization can come at a cost.

Too often, reorganizations are twisted games—even regular rituals—in which insecure, out-of-touch, or untalented executives juggle the lives and careers of their employees. I've often wondered why executives feel such a burning need to reorganize. I've never come up with a satisfying answer, but I think it's because executives at the highest levels often seem to get bored too fast. People at the top are accountable for everything, but responsible for nothing. Day-to-day, they do little actual work. They meet, they plan, they strategize, they pontificate, but they don't sit down and actually produce anything. It's as though they feel that the only way they can earn their hefty salaries is by piecing back their businesses after having smashed them to bits.

Take a step back and analyze the reorganizations you've been involved in. I'll bet that most of them affected middle management and below. If a business is screwed up, a middle-to-low–level reorganization probably isn't the remedy. But in many reorganizations, the lifeblood of the company is drained so that the vampires at the top can continue to feed. Hundreds, sometimes thousands, of middle- and low-level employees can become sacrificial lambs for their esteemed leaders, who are actually responsible for pissing away all the money and negotiating the bad deals that got the company into trouble in the first place.

As an employee I've been involved in at least a half-dozen reorganizations, and as a freelancer I've witnessed several others, and I can say with all honesty that every one of them was poorly planned and executed. While I was doing contract work for an interactive company, they reorganized three times in a single year. It wasn't until the third reorganization that the jackasses responsible for the financial meltdown were finally targeted—and by then it was too late to rehire some of the talented employees who were cut in earlier layoffs.

There's a saying that seems to sum up the whole disturbing reorganization trend: *If it ain't broke, fix it anyway.* That phrase defines many of the major Hollywood studios, where countless script doctors are hired to rewrite screenplays that don't need to be rewritten. It's a phrase that should also be hung in the lobby of every corporation that hires expensive consultants to pinpoint organizational problems that don't exist.

24. GET REAL

The majority of new business ventures fail. Realize, when you start your company, that the odds are stacked against you from the start. Even the Intels, AOLs, and Microsofts of the world are vulnerable. No business is indestructible.

A successful company is a complex engine with many parts. You can't be personally responsible for every facet, every action, of every employee. You can't make two employees who hate each other suddenly bond. You can't rally global financial markets if the economy dips. There are countless factors that lie beyond your control. So don't pin all the blame on yourself if your business fails.

If I had to do it over again, I wouldn't equate business failure with personal failure. When I was younger, I wasn't smart enough or experienced enough to differentiate between the two. In my mind, corporate bankruptcy meant total failure, and failure meant starting over. Some view fresh starts with excitement, but not me. I avoided change with all my might. Plus, corporate bankruptcy probably would have driven me into personal bankruptcy, and the thought of a future with a spotty credit history was unthinkable. These were some of the dark fears that motivated me to press forward when all the odds were against me.

Allowing myself to become paralyzed by the prospect of change and failure was one of my greatest mistakes. But I was lucky—in 1996, what I feared most finally came to pass. I said good-bye to family and friends, walked away from my roots, and started over on the other side of the country. And it wasn't the end of the world, as I'd imagined. In fact, it was exciting and revitalizing. I should have done it much earlier.

There's no shame in failing if you've given it your best effort. Just limit your own personal financial risk, get up every day, keep trying, and don't torture yourself forever if you come up short.

2

MONEY MATTERS

Beware of little expenses; a small leak will sink a great ship.
—Benjamin Franklin

Money is the gas that makes the engine run. But proper financing is only half the battle. You have to know what and what not to do with money once you have it. Unfortunately, my business never had much of it, and what little financing I did have was mismanaged to hell and back. If I had it all over to do again, I'd employ a few of these principles:

25. BE BACKED TO THE HILT

Be properly capitalized or don't start a business. I feel so strongly about this point that I wish I could carve it into a stone tablet and carry it down a mountain somewhere.

Without ample start-up funds, it's doubtful that your business will survive. And if you beat the odds, I guarantee you'll have put a lot of miles on your emotional engine by enduring a long, arduous struggle, a struggle akin to pushing an elephant up a mountain. Trust me—I'm an expert. I spent seven years staring point-blank at an elephant's ass.

In the hope that you'll never get squashed by an elephant,

here are some financing tips based on my own money-raising mistakes:

Take the Venture Capital Test

If you can't attract the attention of legitimate venture capitalists, underwriters, and banks, then you probably don't have a business worth funding. Accept it and get on with your life. It may seem harsh and pessimistic, but it's true.

When I started, I didn't have enough business sense to manage the local Dairy Queen, let alone a software company. No venture capital firm would even consider investing in my business, based on my age and experience. It never even occurred to me that maybe these experts were right. I don't know if it was utter faith, optimism, denial, or stupidity that kept me going. I trudged on and began raising capital from alternate sources. Little did I know that I was opening a can of worms that would plague me for years.

Piecemeal Financing Equals a Neverending Migraine

My early days of raising investment capital were a joke. When venture capitalists rejected my business plan, I did the only thing I could do to keep my vision alive: I approached everyone in town who had money. I pitched the business to rich town doctors, lawyers, distant relatives, friends—anyone with ears. It was difficult, but my tenacity started paying off. A rich local doctor invested and brought along some of his friends. A lawyer and business owner were the next investors; they convinced their buddies to join in.

The good news was that I was indeed raising capital. The bad news was that none of these individuals invested more than $100,000. The result? Within two years, there were more than twenty individual investors in my company, each owning a piece of the pie. And all this piecemeal financing amounted to slightly less than a million dollars. If we had been opening a local retail business or service operation, those funds might have been sufficient to start a company. But I was aiming to launch an international software development and publishing firm. Even in the early days of the software industry, a million dollars wasn't even close to the amount we needed to compete.

When the company faced a cash-flow crisis, my only solution was to put on a dog-and-pony show, dance the save-my-ass tango, and collect another small check from a new investor. I was keeping my business afloat, but I was also making a royal mess of my company's structure by handing out valuable percentages of the business for amounts of money that were probably less than what venture capital firms were spending on their Christmas parties.

The ownership structure became a nightmare, especially when it came time to sell the company. Our corporate bylaws required the unanimous approval of our shareholders to approve the sale, but because our investors were going to receive stock options, not cash, in the company that was acquiring us, it became the hardest sell of my life. Some of the investors threatened to veto the deal unless they were repaid in full. The most troublesome of these shareholders had invested only $8,000 in my company. I was reminded the hard way that the dollar amount of the investment was insignificant; everyone had to vote yes or the deal was blown.

Shortly before it was time for him to cast his proxy vote, this investor started making threats, accusations, and unreasonable demands. After a series of tense and stressful phone calls and meetings, I had no choice but to play the only card I was holding: I threatened to quit. I wasn't just bluffing; I was prepared to pull a Pontius Pilate, wash my hands of the whole mess, walk away, let the company sink, and pit all of the investors against each other in court. Back then, I had rocks as big as church bells. These days, I'm not so brave. My strategy worked. Mr. Unhappy Investor gave in.

Don't take on too many investors. Whether they invest $10 or $10 million, they'll own a piece of your pie and have a say in everything you do. And sadly, you'll be forced to listen.

Make Sure You're Not Breaking the Law

A few years into my career, my attorney alerted me to the fact that I had broken major SEC laws when, instead of selling stock in my company, I sold royalties on our first product. To keep myself out of jail, those royalty agreements had to be converted into stock transactions, which diluted my ownership stake in the company.

Granted, the Clinton-Gore administration got away with fundraising murder in the 1990s, but unless you work in an oval office, follow the advice of a seasoned securities attorney. It isn't difficult to break the law, especially if you're not an expert and you're in desperate need of cash.

If you screw up and commit fraud or corporate tax evasion, you may have to spend a year or so in a federal prison camp. Eglin Air Force Base in Florida—dubbed Club Fed—is one of these white-collar prisons. Before you report to the barracks, the Bureau of Prisons sends you a checklist of what you can and can't bring with you. This is real:

CLOTHING:
- 1 bathrobe (white or gray, no hoods)
- 1 baseball cap (no logos)
- 1 pair of white athletic shoes ($100 maximum) *(No Air Jordans, that's for sure.)*

- 1 pair of specialty shoes (white, black, or combo. $100 maximum) *(What are specialty shoes? Are those for the prison cotillion?)*
- 1 pair of casual shoes
- 1 pair of shower shoes
- 1 pair of slippers (colorless) *(Doesn't everything have a color?)*
- 1 pair of work shoes *(I didn't know you needed special shoes to make license plates. Doesn't this seem like an excessive amount of footwear?)*
- 2 pairs of gym shorts (white or gray)
- 5 pairs of tube socks (white)
- 2 sweatshirts (no logos, no hoods, pullover, cotton)
- 2 pair of sweatpants (cotton, no logos)
- 5 T-shirts/sleeveless undershirts (white or gray, no pockets)
- 7 pairs of underwear (briefs or boxers, white only)
- 5 handkerchiefs (white only)
- *Females:* 5 pairs of stockings/pantyhose
- *Females:* 7 bras and panties

PERSONALLY OWNED ITEMS:
- 1 address book
- 1 non-electric alarm clock
- 1 athletic tote bag (no logo)
- 4 batteries
- 5 books (hard/soft)
- 1 book/reading light
- 1 bowl (plastic/24 oz. or less)
- 1 small calculator *(To calculate how much your net worth is dropping while you're in the slammer.)*
- 2 combs
- 1 combination lock

- 2 pairs of contact lenses
- 1 bottle of contact lens solution
- 1 shaving bag
- 1 cup (plastic)
- 1 set of dentures
- 1 set of earplugs
- 1 box of envelopes
- 2 pairs of eyeglasses *(In case one pair gets smashed in a prison uprising.)*
- 2 eyeglass cases
- 1 hairbrush
- 5 plastic hangers
- 1 set of headphones
- 1 harmonica
- 1 plastic jug (1 gallon)
- 1 laundry bag
- 25 letters
- 1 mirror (plastic/small) *(So much for using a shard to slit the warden's throat!)*
- 2 ballpoint pens
- 2 pencils
- 1 photo album/scrapbook
- 25 photos (no Polaroids or sex photos) *(Why is the establishment so anti-Polaroid?)*
- 2 picture frames (clear plastic)
- 2 decks of playing cards
- 1 Walkman w/earplugs
- 60 stamps
- 1 pair of sunglasses
- 1 thermos (up to 64 ounces)

- 1 large white towel
- 1 watch (not to exceed $100 value)
- 1 watchband
- 1 wedding band (no stones)
- 2 writing tablets
- 1 tennis racket (not to exceed $150 in value) *(There goes graphite!)*
- 1 racketball racket (not to exceed $100 in value)
- *Females:* 1 cosmetic case
- *Females:* 1 pair of earrings
- *Females:* 1 eye shadow kit
- *Females:* 3 lipsticks
- *Females:* 2 makeup/foundation/base

HYGIENE ITEMS:
- 1 container of dental floss
- 1 denture adhesive
- 1 denture brush
- 1 denture cleaner
- 1 denture cup *(There must be some kind of correlation between white-collar crime and a lack of teeth.)*
- 2 deodorants (non-aerosol)
- 1 lens cloth
- 1 set of nail clippers
- 1 razor
- 1 pair of mustache scissors (blunt-tip)
- 1 sewing kit
- 2 bars of soap *(Preferably on a string.)*
- 1 soap dish

- 1 toothbrush
- 1 toothbrush holder
- 2 tubes of toothpaste
- 1 set of blunt-tip tweezers
- *Females:* sanitary items

ITEMS THAT CAN BE OBTAINED AT INMATE'S EXPENSE:

- 2 athletic supporters
- 1 pair of fingerless athletic gloves
- 2 pairs of handball gloves
- 1 mouthpiece for sports *(That's probably a good thing to wear in the shower.)*
- 1 eye protector
- 1 softball glove
- 2 headbands/sweatbands (white only)
- 2 knee wraps
- 2 cans of raquetballs
- 1 can of tennis balls
- 1 weightlifting belt
- 1 pair of weightlifting gloves
- 2 weightlifting wraps *(Good Lord, I could train for the Olympics with all of this stuff!)*
- 1 set of knitting/crochet needles *(To fight your way past the guards.)*
- 1 set of tools for beadwork
- 1 set of yarn, embroidery, hoops/needles *(Maybe you can knit an escape rope.)*
- *Females:* 2 jogging bras

APPROVED RELIGIOUS ITEMS
(TO BE APPROVED BY THE WARDEN):

• Prayer shawl
• Kurda or ribbon shirts
• Medals and pendants
• Beads
• Medicine pouches
• Various types of headwear

OTHER ITEMS:

• 2 cartons of cigarettes
• 1 box of cigars
• 10 packets of instant chocolate
• 1 jar of instant coffee
• 1 jar of Coffee-mate
• 1 package of pipe cleaners
• 1 jar of instant tea
• 10 cans of smokeless tobacco

This may sound like a vacation to some, but it's really not. Being a convicted felon does not open doors in the business world. So familiarize yourself with business law if you plan to own your own business. Pick up some books about business law. Here are some good ones:

West's Business Law: Text and Cases—Legal, Ethical, Regulatory, International, and E-Commerce Environment by Kenneth W. Clarkson (South-Western College Publishing)

155 Legal Do's (and Dont's) for the Small Business by Paul Adams (John Wiley & Sons)

Business Law (Barron's Business Review Series) by Robert W. Eberson and John W. Hardwicke (Barron's Educational Series)

The Entrepreneur's Guide to Business Law by Constance E. Bagley and Craig E. Dauchy (South-Western College Publishing)

Loans Will Kill You

Don't get into doomsday debt to get your organization on its feet. You should be seeking venture capital, not loans. Corporate debt made most of my years in business miserable; the weight of debt wore me down, worried me constantly, kept me awake at night, and made me ill. Of the quarter million dollars I raised, over half of it was in the form of loans that I personally guaranteed. Before I knew it, I was on the hook for much of the company's debt. Talk about an epic, major league mistake.

As your business matures, it's inevitable that you'll need to borrow money at critical junctures (to establish a good credit rating if nothing else), but *make sure your debt-to-capital ratio is sensible—* something like 25 percent debt and 75 percent investment or working capital or 10 percent debt and 90 percent investment working capital. If your debt-to-capital ratio is 50/50 or, in my own case, 40/60, you're in big trouble.

Never be tempted to abuse a credit line. Don't borrow from Peter to pay Paul, and never keep your business alive even one day on strictly borrowed funds.

A company can't grow on quicksand. Too much corporate debt in the early years of a business is just that. Not only can it pull your business under, it can also drag your personal life down with it. Never put your future at risk—only your present.

Don't Bank on Future Cash

Last, *never become dependent on advances against future royalties, or you'll become a slave to a higher power.* Advances are wonderful, but you're fooling yourself if you think it's free money. Nothing is free.

When my company was getting on its feet, a big publisher in the business kept advancing us funds to ease our cash-flow problems. At the time, the publisher's CFO was like our guardian angel, but in the end, he turned out to be our pimp. Once the advances skyrocketed, we were forced—like all desperate whores—to pay off our advances by performing whatever unsatisfying grunt work that our pimp/publisher threw our way.

This is probably the most important lesson in the book. In case you need a summary, here's a quick one: *Piecemeal financing and taking on too much debt in the early days of your business is corporate suicide.*

26. DON'T RISK YOUR UNBORN CHILDREN'S COLLEGE MONEY

Never, ever risk your own money on a business venture. Raise money for your business from outside sources—private investors, venture capital firms, state and federal grants, and so on. What you are bringing to the table of a proposed venture is your commitment, your expertise, your very heart and soul. Don't let anyone try to talk you into putting in your own money as well. *It's a cardinal sin to use your personal savings to fund your business yourself* (unless you're so rich it doesn't matter).

I've been stupid enough to make this mistake more than once. Years ago, I even covered payroll for fifteen employees by writing Discover card checks. It took me four years to recoup that money. You would think I would have learned from such a serious blunder, but just a few short years ago, I did it again.

This time I funded a CD-ROM documentary on the 150-year-old Benedictine monastery and college where I went to school. The campus and grounds are one of my favorite places on earth. The project was sure to be full of history, ghost stories, religious artifacts—topics I loved to sink my teeth into.

After careful calculation, I deemed my risk minuscule. There was no way I couldn't at least break even. After all, the alumni of the college would line up to buy a product with such rich, heartfelt subject matter.

The research was fascinating, and I uncovered all sorts of lost photographs, mysterious stories, and treasures in the monastery archives. It never even entered my mind at the time that I was one of maybe three people this side of Saturn who found Benedictine monks interesting.

Long story short, not even the alumni gave a frog's fat ass about the college's history or seeing old photos of long-dead priests and saints on their computer screens. When all seventy orders were tallied, the verdict became painfully official: I had taken a personal bath and definitely earned a nomination in the Dumb Ass of the Year sweepstakes.

27. A STOCK PRICE DOES NOT A COMPANY MAKE

If you've been lucky enough to take your company public, enjoy the moment, but *don't run your business on the stock price.*

For the average business owner, the initial public offering (IPO) is the Holy Grail of the business quest. It almost always means that the principals in the company have hit the jackpot.

Though I've never personally struck gold on the stock market, I've worked for several public companies and I've experienced the madness of having to maintain and increase a public stock price at the expense of quality, honesty, and dignity.

It's a tale as old as the New York Stock Exchange: A company goes public, the principals take a sip from the well of personal wealth, and they become hopeless money addicts. Fortune proves to be a thirst that is every bit as unquenchable as Dracula's craving for blood. If the company fails to meet Wall Street's expectations, the stock tumbles, and that means no fresh blood for the bloodsuckers who own big blocks of the stock. Now there's no choice: the stock price MUST climb, and damn the consequences!

I've watched companies toss logic and common sense straight out the window to keep an already inflated stock price inching steadily upward. And during the last few years, due to a healthy economy, hundreds, if not thousands, of worthless companies found ways to not only go public, but to trade at several times their actual value. It's all a big house of cards.

Two companies I worked for actually shipped unfinished products just to meet their bogus quarterly projections. And many other companies that aren't quite that desperate often pull another stunt— they'll hack and slash important features out of products in development so they can ship their "shit in a box" for the Christmas shopping season. The customers are the ones being punished, while the owners of the stock keep getting richer. How's that for justice? If the public only knew what the products they were buying were originally designed to be, there would be an uproar.

IPOs are like anything else—they're both good and bad. They're good because large influxes of working capital pour into public companies for future growth. They're bad because the people controlling the large blocks of stock will stop at nothing to protect their personal fortunes. And now that IPOs are as common as hookers on Sunset Boulevard, I have a bad feeling that we're only beginning to scratch the surface of this ugly trend.

28. ALWAYS KNOW WHERE EVERY DAMN NICKEL IS

If you're a principal or an officer in a corporation, always *know the state of your company at all times.* At any given moment, know how much cash the company has, what the payables and receivables are, and what the debt picture looks like.

Don't make the same mistake I made. In my business, I assumed the role of the product guy—the creative one—and allowed others to manage the finances.

While I was doing things like writing dialogue for vampires and reviewing animations of medieval wizards, there were a lot of stupid financial mistakes being made that I was clueless about. People were even enjoying weekend getaways and tropical vacations on company funds. I didn't learn of the magnitude of some of these blunders until the company was about to be sold, but by then it was too late to change anything.

What can I say? I was just plain shit-for-brains stupid to let that happen. Financial managers could have embezzled half the company's money and I would have been none the wiser. Thank God I was never dragged out of the office by the IRS or the police, screaming, "What? What? What did I do?"

I was on the hook for a substantial portion of our corporate debt, so I should have known how every penny was being spent. Instead, I turned a blind eye to the finances because numbers weren't my thing. With my future on the line, numbers should have been not only my thing, but my biggest, baddest, boldest thing of all. I should have been as paranoid as Nixon. I should have demanded to see the books every week. I should have been a righteous, royal nuisance if that's what it took to get a clear picture of our finances.

When money is on the line, trust no one—not your friends, your family, your trusted business associates—not your priest, for that matter. *Know where every nickel is being spent* and don't give *anyone* the opportunity to take advantage of you.

If numbers aren't your thing, then make them your thing. Don't let financial lingo and buzzwords intimidate you. Bottom line, it's all about dollars and cents—how many dollars you have in the bank, how many dollars you owe, and how many dollars are due to flow in. If you feel you need to, take an accounting class, learn to use a spreadsheet program, and read books about business finance.

When one of my friends was getting his master's degrees in literature, he used to send me his required reading list. Even though I had no intention of going to graduate school, I read every novel that those graduate students were reading. Looking back, I should have taken the same approach to my own personal business education. I should have familiarized myself with what MBA students were exploring. If I had, maybe I could have avoided many of my business blunders.

29. BE TIGHT

If you own a business, *hoard money*. Open a special account where you can dump unexpected profits and pretend that the cash isn't there. My company was almost always broke, so this was never an issue for me. But if there had been any cash surpluses, I like to imagine that I would have done this.

Always be cost-efficient. Even if your company has a liquid billion to play with, have strict purchasing guidelines and stick to them. Don't deviate. Be disciplined.

There are a million ways for a business to blow money. Here are a few of my favorites:

Unnecessary Travel

One of the major business mistakes I see again and again is the utterly pointless business trip. With E-mail, telephones, and teleconferencing readily available, why does everyone still travel so much? Sure, there are times when face-to-face contact with clients and associates is a must, but a lot of travel can be avoided—and a lot of money can be saved.

One of the most memorable travel abuses I've ever seen occurred when a company for which I did contract work had a brainstorming session at a four-star ski resort even though the division was drowning in red ink. Layoffs were only months away, but this company saw fit to blow $300,000 rewarding a group of employees who couldn't find their asses on their best day.

I know a lot of people who have journeyed around the globe first-class, all on their company's dime. Do the businesses benefit? Maybe, but I guarantee you not as much as the eager globetrotters doing the traveling.

But who am I to talk? I'm guilty of this sin (except the first-class part). I once spent a week in Japan when I knew there was more of a chance of me capturing Sasquatch than of distributing my products in the Far East. It was, however, a great and memorable trip. I met a lot of interesting people, learned about Japanese culture and business customs, and got turned on to sushi. I even met Joe DiMaggio at the hotel bar. Sure it cost a fortune, but how many times in life do you get to have beers with an American icon, a Hall of Famer—and someone who actually had sex with Marilyn Monroe?

At least when I went on trips, I tried to be thrifty. I've worked with some people who, when spending their own money, stay at motor lodges and eat drive-through value meals, but as soon as they're spending company money, it's a balcony suite at the Ritz, first-class plane tickets, minibar charges, limousine rides, and tables at Spago. Why should any company in business to turn a profit pay for an employee to live like the Sultan of Brunei? A perk or two is one thing, but pampering executives is a wasteful and shameful abuse of corporate funds. Get ye to a Marriot, ye high-living swine.

Unnecessary travel isn't the only way companies piss away cash. How about . . .

Trade Shows

Here, businesses spend fortunes and engage in competitive pissing matches over the size of their booths. Millions of dollars are shoveled into oblivion in an attempt to appease the insecurities associated with corporate "booth envy."

And don't forget the lavish parties and corporate outings that take place during trade show week. One company I designed a game for spent more money throwing a party at the Beverly Hills Hotel than they did on the budget of the product they were showcasing at the party. Then there's . . .

Executive Retreats

I always get a kick out of seminars with titles like "Inroads to Leadership" and "Empowerment 101." What good ever came out of one of these events? Okay, maybe you learned a thing or two at one of them, but did you retain the information? Did you put it into practice?

We should stop calling these events executive retreats and start calling them what they really are—vacations on the house. It's true. An executive conference is like Woodstock for businesspeople. Employees can escape from the office, drink, and golf—and it's all free! If you've been to a retreat and gotten something from it besides a raging hangover, I envy you.

The problem is that none of these seminars teach common sense, and that's the prime ingredient you need to run a business effectively.

And then there's my favorite . . .

The "Morale-Building" Party

IDIOT EXECUTIVE 1
I think we have a major problem. We need to have a meeting—pronto. Call everyone on the executive steering committee and get them in here right now.

IDIOT EXECUTIVE 2
Why? What's the problem?

IDIOT EXECUTIVE 1

The employees seem down. Morale is low.

IDIOT EXECUTIVE 2

Well, we did just lay off half the staff three hours ago. Maybe that has something to do with it.

IDIOT EXECUTIVE 1

Hmm . . . You may be right. . . . Hey, I know. Let's have a party. That'll cheer everyone up.

IDIOT EXECUTIVE 2

That's a great idea! We'll have pizza and ice cream . . . and maybe even games. I'll call the caterer.

For God's sake, can we all end the madness and stop with the parties?! After a layoff and restructuring, morale is low because the employees who are left—feeling like they just survived the Irish potato famine—lament the loss of their friends and coworkers. The last thing they want or need is a phony party with cupcakes and "here's to the future" propaganda. Instead of having a party game like whack the piñata, let employees play "baby seal." That's where they get to beat their incompetent bosses to death with a club. Believe me, that's the only thing that will make any of them feel better.

One company I worked for threw a bogus $200,000 "New Direction for the Future" party, and it was a bust. Everyone left early and went to a local bar for an all-night bitchfest about how piss-poor the company was. At another company, a survivors' party turned downright ugly when a drunken employee shoved the president into a swimming pool. The executive cracked his head on the concrete, and all hell broke loose. To top off the entire tempestuous soiree, another surly employee tried to drive over a coworker. I'll bet that was the only time the police ever had to break up a company picnic.

Bitterness, confusion, and rage bubble over after reorganizations and layoffs. Only time heals wounds. Don't buy into the belief that throwing a sham party will wipe away those frowns.

Tight Doesn't Mean Cheap

One last bit of advice: *Don't be cheap.* Walk the fine line between being truly cost-efficient and being a cheapskate. Don't cross that line, or you'll be despised and disrespected by everyone in and outside of your company. Remember, you get what you pay for.

There's nothing I hate more than when a company nickel and dimes me. The same company that threw a big-bucks party at the Beverly Hills Hotel had the audacity to put me up in the grimiest Manhattan hotel that I've ever seen. The radiator by my bed sounded as if there was a gnome beating the pipes with a crowbar from the inside. This dump was so despicable that they put fake pictures in the hotel brochure.

As soon as my contract ended, I wrote that company off. I'm not asking for the Ritz, but I at least deserve to shower with hot water.

30. DON'T BLOW YOUR WAD ON QUESTIONABLE LICENSES

In my industry, licensing—acquiring the rights to create games based on movies or celebrity names—is a common occurrence. But for every licensing and endorsement deal that turns a profit, there are at least three that don't. *Do your homework before you shell out big bucks to movie studios and celebrities.*

Early in my career, a licensing deal with Marvel Comics put my company on the map. Spider-Man and Captain America are icons that will be around as long as the earth spins, and creating games featuring such recognizable characters is a slam-dunk. The Marvel license, though incredibly expensive, was worth every cent. Without good old Spidey, my company wouldn't have survived.

But licenses and endorsements don't guarantee a product's success. A video game powerhouse began paying exorbitant sums for dozens of movie rights. They struck gold with *Batman*, but guess what happened when they released games in conjunction with flops *Cutthroat Island* and *The Last Action Hero*? They lost millions and learned the hard way that Arnold Schwarzenegger's name on a movie marquee doesn't always guarantee box-office success. Another company in my industry recently took a bath on a *Wild Wild West* game. Even Will Smith, Kevin Kline, and Salma Hayek's magnificent breasts couldn't save that dog of a flick.

In my opinion, it's impossible to predict the next big craze. Most of the time, hits come out of the clear blue sky. Would you have believed me two years ago if I told you that people would be shoving each other to the ground in malls across America to get their hands on furry little rodents that speak gibberish? Probably not, but Furbymania was a sensation. Would you have thought that something as bizarre as Pokémon would become such a monster hit?

If I were going to risk money by acquiring licenses today, I'd bank on the classics (*Star Trek*, *Star Wars*, *Batman*, and so on) and spend money on licenses only after they were proven hits (Harry Potter).

31. GET OUT OF THE TOILET ONE STEP AT A TIME

When dealing with angry bill collectors, be as honest as you can. I respect people who tell me the truth instead of bullshitting me.

Dodging, and lying to, creditors tarnishes your reputation and the reputation of your company.

I've owed far more than I could pay many times in my career. When I tried to dodge and lie, I ended up feeling like a schmo. Maybe it was the ghosts of all those nuns from Catholic school whispering in my ear, but I truly did suffer from a guilty conscience. No amount of alcohol could drown it out. No distraction could make me forget. The thought of unpaid bills and the voices of angry creditors kept me up at night.

My blood pressure skyrocketed every time the sheriff walked into the office carrying a new lawsuit. Ultimately, I came to the conclusion that the only way I could continue to function in business without becoming a raging alcoholic was just to be honest; I came clean with every creditor. I found that most (not all) of them were willing to cooperate with me if I adhered to a realistic payment plan. In a way, I had them all over a barrel and they knew it. If they sued me, they would be wasting money because even if they won a judgment, there were other creditors in line and really nothing of value in my company to liquidate except computers, which were depreciating by the minute. If I declared corporate bankruptcy, the creditors would be lucky to get ten cents on the dollar. At least a fair payment plan would keep me out of bankruptcy and get them some, if not all, of their money back over time.

With my new approach to paying my business's bills honestly, I could sleep at night. I began to retire debt a dollar at a time. Even if it was only a few hundred dollars a month, I worked hard to keep my word and crack the egg—the magnificent three-story egg—that I had foolishly allowed myself to lay.

To the creditors, it looked like an honest effort; my credibility was enhanced. It took years to pay off my suppliers, but I did it. I could have gone the bankruptcy route and washed my hands clean, but I didn't. I'm still proud of that.

However, when creditors refused to cooperate and I only had enough money to pay either my employees or my bills, my philosophy was to . . .

32. PAY THE EMPLOYEES FIRST

If you can't pay your employees—the lifeblood of your company— you're out of business. Period. Don't delay the inevitable. Declare bankruptcy, liquidate your business, and don't wait until payday to pull the rug out from under your employees. It's not fair to ask anyone to work for free, so don't string your people along. And don't promise your employees two paychecks next payday if they'll just cut you a break and let this payday slide. This is not only a deceitful scheme, it's a desperate one. When faced with the dilemma of having just enough money to pay either my employees or my towering stack of bills—or even my payroll taxes—I always paid my employees first, even when I had to make advances against credit cards to cover the payroll. The fact that I was even in such a dark and hopeless place was a major mistake in itself, but that mistake would have compounded a thousandfold if I had asked or expected any of my people to work for free.

On payday, be sure to pay yourself along with your employees. *Never work for free.* During the cash-flow crisis where I was writing credit card checks, I didn't pay myself for four months. BIG MISTAKE! If you can't swing paying yourself and it's not hurting your productivity, my hat's off to you. Skipping payday never made me feel like a hero; it made me angry, bitter, and unproductive.

After you've paid yourself and your employees, *the next most important thing to pay is your payroll taxes*. I made the mistake of letting mine slip during my worst financial crisis, and it was an epic mistake. I learned firsthand that the IRS will not listen to excuses or forgive and forget. As an officer of your corporation, you'll take the heat. When the IRS came after me, they produced a laundry list of tax crimes that I would be charged with if I didn't adhere to their strict payment schedule. If I was even an hour late with one of the payments, they promised to close down the company and arrest me. I had to beg and borrow to meet the IRS's schedule, but I paid Uncle Sam and I'll never butt heads with him again.

When it comes to your bills, *do the best you can*. Don't put your operation at risk by parting with precious capital to appease angry bill collectors. Be honest with your creditors; attempt to pay them over time, but realize that if they refuse to cooperate, you'll have no choice but to duck and hide until the crisis passes.

Once I subcontracted a young guy to program a game. I owed him several thousand dollars, but there was no way I could pay him, at least not for a couple of months. I tried to be honest and negotiate a payment schedule, but he refused to cooperate. I had enough money to pay him or pay my employees (about a dozen at the time), but not both. I put him on my back burner and tuned him out. He pulled all of the usual stunts to get his money—calling me constantly, clogging up my fax machines with invoices (this was before E-mail), and sending me letters full of legalese, but I ignored him.

Then an unexpected event caught me off guard. The programmer's father hopped on a plane from Canada to collect his son's money. Without warning, I got a call from Proud Papa, who told me he was in a hotel a few miles away and wanted directions to my office. Knowing full well that there was no way I could cut Papa a check, I had to think of something fast. I immediately sent most of the employees out for an early lunch on the company. I turned off the lights and computers for effect just as Papa walked in. He immediately noticed that the office was deserted. I lied and told him that I had been forced to lay off my staff and was in the process of declaring bankruptcy.

The illusion worked. Papa believed my story and, figuring that his son was never going to see a cent, returned to Canada on the afternoon flight. He even had the class and human decency to console me on the loss of my business on his way out.

You may believe that I was a rotten SOB to look this man in the eye and lie. I'm not proud of it, but times were desperate and I did what I had to do to get Papa—and all of the other creditors who were hounding me—off my back so that my employees could keep working.

It took a long time, but eventually I paid the programmer. I'm sure that after having written his money off, he and his father were pleasantly surprised to find a check in the mail.

Pay your bills the best you can, but above all else, keep a healthy output of quality labor flowing. As long as your productivity remains high, you'll have a fighting chance of surviving even the worst cash-flow crisis.

33. LIEN ON ME

If your company extends large amounts of credit to clients, you want to ensure that you're considered a secured creditor. As an unsecured creditor your company has no right to property or collateral owned by the debtor. Thus, if your company gets stiffed, you'll have to go to court to try to recover your money. The problem is that there are usually a lot of other companies and individuals standing in line waiting for their money as well, so you'll be lucky to recoup ten cents on the dollar.

A secured creditor, on the other hand, has a specific property right called a security interest or lien, under state bankruptcy laws. Though these laws vary from state to state, the fundamental procedure is basically the same: The secured creditor can typically recover what is owed by legally seizing assets or collateral *without going to court.*

In order to become a secured creditor, file a UCC-1 financing statement with central local and state authorities. Again, this practice varies by state, so my advice would be to contact your local county recorder or your corporate attorney to inquire further about this process.

Always insist on becoming a secured creditor if your business is lending money to another company, or if you personally lend money to another company, or if you personally lend money to an individual or business. By legally being able to file a lien against your debtors, you'll be first in line (second in line behind the IRS if unpaid taxes are outstanding) to collect your money if the person or company you lend money to declares bankruptcy and is forced to liquidate.

A venture capital firm once made a $50,000 loan to my company. Unbeknownst to the other investors, this firm had filed for a UCC-1, and this gave them the right to seize, hold, or sell my company's property if the loan was not repaid or if the company was acquired. When our company was sold, the buyer had no choice but to pay off the venture capitalist's loan, thanks to their insightful business strategy.

The other investors who loaned money to my company didn't receive the same treatment. Instead of cash, they were forced to accept stock warrants in consideration of their loans. Many of my investors were livid when they learned that the venture capital firm was going to get its money, but there wasn't a thing they could do about it. If they had filed UCC-1's after they made their loans, they would have received the same treatment.

Again, consult your corporate attorney to ensure that you're considered a secured creditor in all your financial dealings. The legal right to file a lien assures you of at least getting a healthy portion of your loan back if trouble erupts.

3

HOW TO MANAGE MANAGING

A boss creates fear, a leader confidence. A boss fixes blame, a leader corrects mistakes. A boss knows all, a leader asks questions. A boss makes work drudgery, a leader makes it interesting. A boss is interested in himself or herself, a leader is interested in the group.

—Russel H. Ewing

There is something that is much more scarce, something finer far, something rarer than ability. It is the ability to recognize ability.

—Elbert Hubbard

Though no two businesses are alike, the general company atmosphere is almost always driven by the personalities of the top managers. They set the general tone that makes a workplace a mean, competitive environment or a positive, nurturing one.

Without good managers, a company will quickly find itself adrift in a sea of mediocrity. That's where I was floating for much of my career, especially the early years. Now that I've been away from day-to-day management for a few years, I've had time to look back and evaluate my management mistakes.

When I think about management, one fundamental phrase sums it up for me: *Do unto others.* Work out conflicts fast. Do it honestly and quickly, or the cancer will spread and become terminal. It's not that hard: Put yourself in your employees' shoes and see issues from their perspective, as well as your own. That's real leadership in my book—to stand by your decisions and not be swayed, but to be respectful enough to appreciate someone's viewpoint even when you disagree with it. It sounds so corny, but there's still no better way to resolve a conflict. If you honestly employ this age-old strategy during negotiations, conflict management, and personnel issues, you'll be respected.

Respect is a critical management fundamental. There's no way you can be an effective manager unless you've earned the respect of your employees. With respect comes loyalty, and loyalty is as critical to a manager's survival as oxygen and water.

What most bad managers never grasp is yet another fundamental: *Respect is a two-way street.* To earn respect, managers must be willing to show respect. Sure, this sounds like it came straight out of the pages of any one of a hundred management books, but it's one of those almighty business commandments that's really true. Not everyone you extend courtesy and respect to will return it, but at least you can demand respect if you're giving it.

There are a million and one ways you can treat your employees with disrespect. You can demean them, bully them, insult them, pressure them, pit them against each other, lie to them, harass them, threaten them, dangle their jobs over the abyss, and on and on. There are also an equal number of ways that employees can feel you're treating them disrespectfully even when you're not. You can cut them out of meetings, force them into giving useless presentations, move their cubicles without telling them, forget to invite them to an off-site meeting or trade show, and so on.

Management is a tricky, complex, grueling game with no fixed rules. Bringing diverse groups of people—all with their own personality quirks and agendas—together to focus on and accomplish a common goal is a mighty task. Handling, juggling, and sometimes dropping the hopes of other human beings is an awesome responsibility.

While almost anyone can be a manager, only a very small percentage can be good managers. The best managers care about themselves and other people. They're the hearts and souls of their organizations. Patient, conscientious, open-minded—they're a rare, priceless breed.

If and when I ever manage again, I'll employ some of the major remedies to the management mistakes that I've made and watched others make:

34. YOU'RE NOT STALIN

Being promoted to a management position does not give you the right to become a dictator. The business world is already jam-packed with tyrants; there's no need for fresh talent.

When I think about how many nice people have gone on to become total pricks after they've become managers, I look skyward and pray for a UFO to swoop down and carry me off this idiotic world.

The transformation from human being to dictatorial unholy terror is usually a rapid one. Normally, when feebleminded newborn dictators assume power, they explode out of the gate and toss their freshly gained weight around without a shred of grace or savvy. Within days, dictators are behaving despicably, abusing and offending everyone in their path. Before they cash their first paycheck, most dictators have amassed a laundry list of enemies, but they are too self-absorbed to even know or care. By acting undiplomatically, tyrants believe they are earning respect, but they're too blind to realize that the only thing they're earning is the unanimous hatred of everyone forced to tolerate them. They especially raise the ire of coworkers with whom they came up in the ranks.

For dictators, the abuse of power—the need to control the lives and careers of their employees—becomes a sport. Every trace of humanity is burned away long before their first anniversary on the job. Dictators wrap up their entire identities in their corporate positions; they seldom have personal lives or responsibilities outside of the office. Work is their heaven and their hell.

Do I exaggerate? I think not. I'll stand by my personality profile of an office fascist. I've worked for and suffered under several dictatorial corporate regimes. I've even started down the path to becoming a dictator myself, before regaining my senses and my humanity just in the nick of time. How did I do that? I looked in the mirror, asked myself questions, and answered them honestly.

Where do you fall on the scale between being a Mr. Nice Guy/Gal and a dictator? I hope you're somewhere in the middle, but there's only one way to find out. Carefully consider the following questions and rate yourself from 0 to 3 (0 = never, 1 = rarely, 2 = often, and 3 = always).

- Do you threaten employees to get your way? (See 35, "Don't Dangle a Job Like a Carrot on a String")

- Do you tell employees how to do their jobs and force them to make unnecessary changes to their work to appease you? (See 36, "Not Every Schmuck Can Do Every Job")
- Do you make unrealistic demands and burn out your employees? (See 38, "Trust the Force, Luke")
- Do you stand over your employees' shoulders and exert pressure on them while they work? (See 39, "Don't Make Unrealistic Demands")
- Do you blow your top? (See 41, "Don't Lose Your Cool")
- Do you force other people to do your dirty work? (See 44, "Get Your Own Hands Dirty")
- Do you refuse to shut up during meetings? (See 50, "Shut Up and Listen")
- Do you betray your employees' trust? (See 52, "Just Shut Up")
- Do you lie and withhold information from your employees? (See 54, "Speak the Truth")
- Are you a negative force who brings everyone down? (See 55, "Don't Preach Doom")
- Do you break your promises? (See 56, "Keep Promises")
- Do you change the rules once they've been set? (See 58, "Tell Them What You Want")
- Do you make your employees feel worthless by trying to motivate them with negative feedback? (See 59, "Don't Criticize a Job Well Done—Praise It")
- Do you discriminate? (See 65, "You're Not Archie Bunker")

All right, tally up those scores. My score was 15. At my worst, I might have reached the low 20s. How about you? When you have a number, let's analyze it.

0–15

Mr. Nice Guy/Gal. You're too nice for your own good. The closer you are to zero, the more likely you'll be eaten alive on the job. You can't be a saint and expect to survive in a politically charged corporate environment. Everyone needs to have a little dictator in them, so toughen up and quit worrying about being liked.

16–30

Seasoned and Savvy. This is the ideal range for management success. On one side of the seesaw is Mr. Nice Guy/Gal; on the other side sits a dictator. You have to balance yourself directly in the center of this seesaw. You can't shift all your weight to one side or the seesaw tips, and when it slams to the ground in either direction, you're in trouble. Some days, you need to be a little more dictatorial than nice. Other days, vice versa. I like to have one foot (and one foot only) leaning toward Stalin, with the other foot firmly rooted in the dead center of the seesaw. That's how I balance myself.

31–39

Pushing Your Luck. I sure as hell wouldn't want to work for you. You're a mean one, Mr. Grinch, and no doubt you have a list of enemies that would make Nixon blush. I'll bet there's a bull's-eye on your back right now. Sooner or later, you'll wear out your welcome, and when you do, the people you've abused will be waiting to pounce on and devour you.

Like Scrooge, wake up before it's too late. There's still a chance to save your dark-hearted soul. As long as you haven't cracked the magic number 40, a ray of hope still shines. If Darth Vader can come back from the dark side, so can you.

40–42

No Man's Land. You, dear friend, are a complete asshole. You create nothing but misery. If you bought this book and I've just insulted you, take it back. I don't want you reading it anyway. You are a hopeless, insecure, cowardly scourge on the business world. You should be disemboweled and strung up by your toes.

Bask in your momentary glory, because I have three words for you: IT WON'T LAST. And if by chance you're proud of your 40+ badge of shame and seek to become the most evil manager ever, forget it. That title belongs to a guy I'll call Peter Principle, the worst manager I've ever met. I name Peter in tribute to Dr. Laurence J. Peter's classic book *The Peter Principle*, which postulates that people in business end up getting promoted one level above their competency level.

Peter Principle shouldn't have been managing the Blue Light Special at Kmart, but somehow he was a senior-level manager for a big Silicon Valley company. He was responsible for several projects and had more than forty employees reporting directly to him.

I'm not exaggerating when I said that Peter did *everything* wrong. He would sign off on impossible schedules and then drive his employees to the brink of madness by forcing them to meet unrealistic deadlines. He constantly threatened to fire his employees and even threatened bodily injury (castration was his favorite) when he got furious. He would expect team members to work around the clock and on weekends even though he was nowhere to be found (he was a new father, after all). When approaching deadlines worried him, Peter called his employees at home after midnight and asked them why they were sleeping. He smashed staplers and other office supplies for dramatic effect when he wanted to illustrate the seriousness of a deadline. He was even stupid enough to invite his employees out for drinks, guzzle booze until he was half-blind, and then spin vulgar yarns until he offended everyone in his presence.

I'll be referring to Peter a lot in this section, but I won't divulge his fate until chapter 4, "In the Trenches." I promise you he didn't die a happy corporate death.

Okay, now that we know where we all stand in the great management scheme, let's proceed.

35. DON'T DANGLE A JOB LIKE A CARROT ON A STRING

You'll never motivate your employees by threatening to take away their livelihoods. Maybe you'll scare them enough to get your way, but you'll never bring out the best in anyone who is a nervous wreck because he doesn't know if he'll have a job in a month.

Dangling jobs over the abyss is an ugly strategy that is purposely employed by top-level managers in some of the biggest corporations in the world.

The owner of one of the companies I worked for was a master of the blind threat. It never occurred to him to motivate employees positively. It was never: "We need this game done by November 1. I know we can do it, and if we do, the company will really be in strong shape."

Instead, it was: "If the game isn't done by November 1, there will be layoffs." Never anything specific about what kind of layoff, how many layoffs, when the layoffs might be—just layoffs. Sometimes he was bluffing; other times he wasn't.

This manager thought he was lighting a fire under us, but he was only setting a blaze under himself. Whenever he pulled this stunt, it didn't motivate our employees or make them work harder; it made them look for other jobs.

If you threaten to fire your employees unless you get your way, stop it. If you work for someone who employs this tactic, call a good employment recruiter and find another job as quickly as you can. There are enough scary things in life—your job security shouldn't be one of them.

36. NOT EVERY SCHMUCK CAN DO EVERY JOB

Respect the boundaries between job positions. In my industry, the release of a new game requires the combined efforts of producers, artists, programmers, creative writers, musical composers, sound effects designers, and game testers. No one component is more important than another. The producer or project leader is not skilled in every area of production. That would be impossible. Likewise, most creative writers can't program, most artists can't write, and most programmers can't animate or compose music. So much valuable time is wasted on projects when someone from one job discipline sticks his nose in an area that's not his forte just because he has a "cool idea." When someone who doesn't know what he's talking about tells someone else how to do his job, the team begins to splinter. Resentment and backstabbing follow; a bubbling tension soon pervades the entire office.

One of my personal pet peeves as a freelance designer and writer is when a producer demeans my creative role on a project by allowing other team members (artists, programmers, even accountants) without writing or storytelling skills to contribute ideas in design brainstorming sessions just to promote teamwork. Sure, thinking up stories and characters is more fun than bean counting (for most of us), but why should I listen to an accountant tell me how to write a story any more than she should listen to me tell her how to itemize deductions? I don't claim to know how to animate or write programming code or compose music. Why must everyone insist that they are experts in interactive fiction? I'm the person with forty-plus games under my belt, but that fact is completely ignored just so that everyone can enjoy the fun part of developing a computer game. Most often, after one of these free-for-all brainstorming sessions, I'm left with nothing but a headache and a handful of plot ideas that feel like they were lifted from a twenty-five-year-old episode of *Mannix*.

37. PISS IN YOUR OWN WEEDS

The dictatorial project leaders I've worked with have stepped all over their employees' toes by forcing their own ideas down their subordinates' throats. They demean the talents and skills of their workers by turning a deaf ear and insisting that they know best. Lenny DaVinci, a creative director I worked with, comes to mind. He was not above pontificating on the art of prose to a roomfull of professional writers. He told artists how and what to draw. Though he had Van Gogh's ear for music, he would hum little ditties to composers and order them to "do something good like that." The shallow products that were released under Lenny's regime mirrored his trifling vision and talent.

Everyone wants to feel appreciated, to have their egos stroked. *As a manager, learn to make suggestions, sometimes firm suggestions, not demands.* If you're a good manager, you're going to know exactly what you want and how you want it done. But you should adopt a nondictatorial approach. Even when it's your way or the highway, respect what people have to say. Encourage ideas and input from your subordinates even when you don't want them. Learn to give and take. Study the people working under you. Question them. Get to know them. Learn what buttons motivate and persuade them and what buttons raise their ire. Help mold their egos so that you'll know what to do and say to value their work, even when their ideas are rejected. As long as you listen to input thoughtfully and avoid belittling your employees for having opinions, you'll be managing well.

Don't allow employees to criticize the efforts of their coworkers in an effort to make themselves look better. Most people take pride in their work. No one enjoys having a spotlight shined on his faults by someone who has a laundry list of faults of his own.

During my last management stint, the person who always shined the brightest light on others was a computer programmer I'll call the Dungeon Troll. He was a truly miserable creep, with a beard full of crumbs and yellow armpit stains on his T-shirts. Not only was he a *Dungeons and Dragons* devotee, he even resembled a Tolkienesque gnome. For five years, the Dungeon Troll was a thorn in my side, a true horror to manage. He had countless irritating habits, including a penchant for pestering female employees, but probably the most grating thing he did was to come into my office and point out the professional and personal shortcomings of the members of the project team while ignoring the fact that he was always behind schedule. He held up a mirror to everyone but his ugly self.

38. TRUST THE FORCE, LUKE

The best executive is the one who has sense enough to pick good men to do what he wants done, and self-restraint enough to keep from meddling with them while they do it.
—Theodore Roosevelt

Let your employees do their jobs. Give them the chance to succeed or fail and don't put undue pressure on them, or you'll burn them out.

I worked with one manager who was the walking definition of

the word paranoid. He would literally stand over the shoulders of employees and remind them that if they didn't meet their deadlines, the company was dead. He couldn't sit still. He obsessed and worried and asked employees ten times a day if they were still on schedule. Before an artist could even submit an animation or a writer could finish a paragraph, he was reviewing their work behind their backs. He became belligerent, demanding revisions while work was still in progress. Several people cracked under the pressure. An equal number got fed up and quit. It's impossible to do every job in a corporation yourself. At some point you have to take a leap of faith and let people do what you hired them to do. Let your employees breathe and stay out of their way, or you'll end up losing them.

39. DON'T MAKE UNREALISTIC DEMANDS

Don't expect your employees to work miracles. Don't create impossible schedules and then expect your employees to drive themselves to the brink of nervous breakdowns trying to meet them.

I'm guilty of this mistake. In 1991, I was responsible for a game I had completely underestimated. Rather than cut features out of the product, I pressured the team to work around the clock. I did my best to lead by example and live in the office with them. The company even paid for hotel rooms and meals for some of the employees who had long commutes. If employees weren't working at night or on weekends, I gave them grief. This work schedule lasted the entire summer. In August, one of the programmers finally cracked. His mother came from out of state and picked him up, and I never saw him again.

What an ass I was. I should have respected that while I didn't have a social life, the other employees probably did. Luckily, we were all young, single kids. If I had pulled such a inconsiderate stunt with someone older, someone with a family, I probably would have been sued.

What comes around definitely goes around. A few years ago I was doing a contract job for a game company, and the fascist project manager would not lighten up during my six-week design tenure. Paranoid that my design might prove too difficult to engineer, she hounded me hourly. The Succubus, as I'll call her, was relentless. On the first Sunday of the NFL season, I settled into my sofa and picked up the phone to speed-dial Domino's Pizza, but it rang. It was the Succubus. She asked if she could come to my house to discuss the design document just so that she could "put her mind to rest." Looking back, I should have said a thousand things, "NO!" being the most obvious. What did I do? Dumb ass that I was, I agreed.

As soon as the Succubus showed up, the air conditioner went on the fritz. The temperature outside soared to a hundred degrees, and I must have sweated off ten pounds over the course of the nine hours she sat at my kitchen table obsessing about graphs full of cartoon character information. I not only missed the games, I missed *King of the Hill* and, most disturbingly, *The Simpsons.* A few weeks later, I delivered the document and all was well, but I will not rest until I get even by stealing one of the Succubus's Sundays. Someday.

40. DON'T FLASH YOUR WAD

Don't flaunt the fact that you make more money than your subor-dinates. Money is a major source of frustration for most people. Those who have more of it become targets for that frustration.

If you're the boss, don't run around and tell everyone to come out-side and check out your new Porsche. You may think you're impressing the troops, but truth be known, your employees are probably fantasizing about how they'd like to key your door.

Don't invite employees for a party at your new house if you're living in a palace. Don't describe your tropical timeshare or boast about how your stock portfolio is bursting at the seams.

Once, when I was in the process of buying a car, I let everyone within earshot know it. Big mistake, since the car cost more than some of the employees' yearly salaries. The first few weeks I drove that car into the parking lot, I caught many stares of resentment. When I bought a house a few years later, I used my head and kept quiet about it.

41. DON'T LOSE YOUR COOL

Watch your temper. Loose cannons make everyone nervous. I mentioned in 34, "You're not Stalin," how Peter Principle used to scream for dramatic effect when he wanted to shake up his employees. His loss of control came back to haunt him and was a major factor in his demise, as you'll read about in the next chapter.

I worked alongside one manager—I'll call him Roy Rage—who had the worst and most erratic temper of anyone I've ever known. Once Roy came so unglued at work that he smashed a wall with his fist. It looked as if a hand grenade had gone off in the office, and every employee who witnessed the tirade lost total respect for him.

At one of Roy's parties (with most of the employees present), he and his girlfriend got into an argument and retired to the bathroom to duke it out in private. When someone had the audacity to knock because his back teeth were floating, this guy smashed the door down in another Hulk-like rage. The party ended instantly, and once again, employees were left looking at each other quizzically, wondering what kind of lunatic their boss was.

During a cash-flow crisis, Roy got so furious at a vendor who was calling for his money that he threatened to "rip his heart out and show it to him before he died." The vendor called me a few minutes later and told me that if I didn't rein in this manager and make him apologize, he would call the police and press charges.

Peter Principle and Roy Rage are not leaders, they're clowns. Psychotic behavior doesn't motivate people; it lets them know what an idiot they're working for. It also alerts them that they have to find work in a more stable environment.

Employees are looking for a calm voice of reason, not the screams of a toddler who should be spanked and sent to bed without his supper. When you fly off the handle, you lose your credibility as a leader. Be calm. Act without emotion. Act as if everything is under control, even when it's not.

42. SET A GOOD EXAMPLE

If you want people to stay late or work on weekends, then you'd better be there right alongside them. For a couple of years in the late 1980s, I had a bad habit of coming in late every morning because I stayed up far too late at night. On my average workday, I would arrive at ten in the morning and leave at nine or ten at night. Then I'd go home and stay up until two or three watching movies or reading. Though I was putting in more than my share of hours, the employees could not overlook the fact that I came in at ten when they had to be there by eight-thirty. I'm sure it looked to them as if I was abusing my power. I was stubborn, but two things finally drove the point home. First, I heard through the grapevine that every morning at nine, some of the employees would joke around about who was going to leave me a wake-up call. Second, when my prank Secret Santa gift at the Christmas party was an alarm clock, everyone enjoyed a good laugh, and I finally got the message. Old habits were hard to break, but I made it a point to alter my routine so that I was there in the early hours with everyone else.

On a similar note, never be the first person to leave at night. Employees tend to stay later if their boss is still in the building.

43. THEY SHOULD SWEAT WHEN THEY HEAR YOU COMING

In business, it's my strong opinion that it's better to be feared than loved. My natural personality leans toward Mr. Nice Guy, but in management positions, Mr. Nice Guys get taken advantage of. I was never blind to the fact that I was often played for a sap because I was too nice. Still, it bothered me. After I sold my company, I vowed to do it differently when the next opportunity presented itself.

When I began managing a new group in 1993, I knew I needed a new image. I would have to don some sort of costume to mask my Mr. Nice Guy predisposition. Who could I be? Macchiavelli, Michael Corleone, Franklin Roosevelt, Steve Jobs, Colonel Sanders? Then I realized that I didn't have to look for a costume so far from home. I decided I'd be like my father. When I was a kid, my dad didn't say much, but when he did, it was important and I listened. He never had to badger me or chase me around the house or take a belt to me—ever. I feared him, and I knew better than to test him. When I stepped out of line an inch, all he had to do was look me in the eyes and drop his voice an octave and my knees shook. Over the years, my dad softened, but during my early childhood, when a lot of kids find a way to wrap their parents around their fingers, my dad had my ticket punched.

With my dad as my role model, I found an *effective middle ground between being a pushover and a ballbreaker*. I strove to convey a strong, no-nonsense image—mysterious and a little aloof, but always approachable, humorous, and decent. To my inner circle, I didn't change. You can't fool the people who know the real you. But to new employees, I was my dad, and I wore my costume with success. Newcomers never knew quite what to make of me. Sometimes my door was open, sometimes closed. Sometimes I listened to people gripe, other times I silenced them. Some days I smiled, some months I didn't. I was never threatening or mean, but I was also no cheerleader. Employees definitely thought twice before crossing the line, and when they did try to take advantage of me, I didn't turn a blind eye. Sometimes I was still taken advantage of, but it was a lot less often than when I was Mr. Nice Guy.

But be careful that you don't go overboard with the tough stuff. A film producer I know makes it a point to fire someone from the crew during the first week of a shoot just to get everyone's attention and respect. He picks his victim strictly based on physical appearance (usually a less-than-stunning female) and berates her every five minutes. He points out fault after fault (real and imagined) until finally, comfortable that he has captured everyone's utmost attention, he fires her in front of everyone.

When I worked with him, the poor script supervisor was the target of his wrath. Though she wasn't the brightest lightbulb in the chandelier, she certainly didn't deserve the producer's abusive wrath. It was awful to watch her be humiliated and fired in front of her peers. You might think that this producer was a horrifying man, but he wasn't. Away from the set, he was charming and funny. But to this day, he has a firm belief that he won't be taken seriously until he lops someone's head off.

44. GET YOUR OWN HANDS DIRTY

If you want to be a good leader, a respected manager, have the guts to do your own dirty work. When it comes to disciplining or firing employees, don't pawn it off on others. I really have a personal pet peeve—no, that's too mild, I have a personal red-blooded hatred—for cowards who will do anything to avoid conflict. I'll tell you why.

I watched the president of a company I worked for pull an utterly cowardly act. Ever the cutting-edge visionary, this moron proclaimed (incorrectly) in 1995 that education software was a dead market. I guess he never heard of Sesame Street, but that's not the point. He decided to cut our company's education division. He called in the manager of the education department and ordered her to fire her employees, with vague assurances that she would remain with the company in a new capacity. Reluctantly, she undertook the painful, grimy task of laying off all of the employees one at a time. After the dirty work was done, he fired her the next day.

This same executive, along with his boss, the CEO of the company, cooked up another whopper of a yellow-bellied scheme to avoid having to fire another employee themselves. This time, the president announced to a handful of us that the CEO had fired Bob, a popular employee from one of our branch offices. One of the employees in our office called Bob to express his condolences, but Bob had no idea what he was talking about. That's because Bob hadn't actually been fired yet! These gutless executives knew that by announcing the firing, one of us was bound to call Bob and break the bad news. The paranoid duo hit a double jackpot. Not only did they get someone else do their dirty work for them by calling Bob, they also got to sniff out a potential traitor, because whoever made the call was a friend of the enemy.

Being a boss means that you'll have to do a hell of a lot of things you don't want to do, but it comes with the territory. It's why you get paid the big bucks. It's why you have a bigger office and a parking space. Live with it. Earn your keep and quit pawning off the unpleasantries.

45. THE HALLWAY BULLETIN BOARD CAN DO SOME OF THE DIRTY WORK FOR YOU

Good managers stay on top of their projects from day one until the product hits the store shelves. *Efficient leaders oversee a smooth production effort by creating realistic schedules and making sure the team adheres to these schedules religiously.*

Many times when I was overseeing projects, I felt more like a baby-sitter than a manager, especially when the project teams grew to more than twenty people. It was difficult to keep everyone on track. I made the mistake of accepting excuses. Instead of managing with an iron fist, I managed with silk gloves. My schedules became as worthless as scrap paper because there weren't consequences for failing to meet them. Products began to slip off schedule, and once that happens, marketing dollars get wasted, salespeople are left with egg on their faces, and financial projections get blown. It's a snowball effect, a downward spiral into the pit of corporate failure. I tumbled into that pit more than once in my career.

When I got a fresh start in 1993, I thought about how I could prevent myself from being sucked into that pit again. While I was watching the movie *Full Metal Jacket*, I got an idea. Remember Pyle, the fat, stupid Marine who kept screwing up? Remember how the drill sergeant quit punishing him and started punishing the other members of the platoon? Remember how those other platoon members finally got fed up enough to beat Pyle with bars of soap wrapped in towels in the middle of the night? Hmm . . .

I thought about that movie and did two things to make sure that schedules were taken more seriously. First, I linked employee bonuses to team completion, not individual completion of job tasks. Everyone got a bonus or no one did. Second, I made the entire team aware of each other's schedules by posting them in a hallway by the restrooms, a place everyone had to walk by at least once or twice a day.

Sure, my plan was colored with a dab of communist red, but it worked. My job suddenly became easier. I didn't have to ride my employees as hard as I did before I posted the schedules. I wasn't creating the pressure. The new bonus plan and public schedules were doing that for me. If anyone, including me, fell off schedule, the entire team became aware of it. And with bonus money on the line, the losers who couldn't hold up their end not only got pressure from me, but from the other team members as well.

Allowing public schedules to create the pressure is a hell of a lot better than having to babysit employees and listen to any one of a thousand of their lame excuses for failing. Try it. I think you'll like the results.

46. THIS AIN'T NO NIGHTCLUB

Watch how much you drink (or smoke, shoot, or snort) in front of your employees. If you're not careful, alcohol can become one of your worst enemies in business. Get drunk with your friends and family, but not your coworkers and especially not your employees. I wish I could say that I never made this mistake, but I'm guilty as charged. I never met a drink I didn't like. But no matter how hard I try to justify it, I can't deny the fact that business and booze *do not* mix. I've made countless business mistakes under the influence of the devil's urine. I could probably write a volume on this topic, but I'll just sum up my thoughts with a couple of simple equations:

alcohol + alcohol = one drink too many
one drink too many + drinking with employees = loose lips
loose lips + your blind trust = ammunition for your enemies
ammunition for your enemies = your ass

I have an ongoing love–hate relationship with alcohol. I love how it takes the edge off a bad day, how it helps me relax, how it makes bad situations a little funnier and definitely more bearable. But I hate how it flips a little switch in my brain that puts my mouth into maximum overdrive. Nowadays, I think I've grown tired of hearing myself talk, but when I was in my twenties, dear God, how I loved to drink with my employees and business associates and talk them to death. That was the essence of my social life. I would tell people who were working for me or who I was doing business with everything about me, my business, the company's finances, who I liked, who I thought was hot, who I wanted to fire . . . blah, blah, blah! And many of my employees, hungry for inside information, clung to my every drunken, slurred word. I showed my cards to everyone who wanted to see them—gave away my edge. No one should have known a thing about my business, or me, but I naively thought that everyone was my friend.

Though I chattered endlessly when I drank, luckily, I never did anything too shameful in front of my employees. I guess the dumbest thing I ever did with business associates was during a trade show in

Chicago. I walked back to the hotel with some of my employees after a heavy-duty drinking and bitching session. For some reason that only the god Bacchus probably understands, I ended up stepping right into a fountain. I was still wearing my shoes and socks. I tossed a quarter in the water and wished aloud that my feet were dry. Everyone got a good laugh, but for years, that story was told to every new employee as if it was a requirement of the training program.

And though I made many drunken blunders, no one took this mistake to greater heights more than a guy I once worked with whom I'll call Wally Whiskeybreath. When I was away on vacation, Wally fired three employees for "insubordination." That night, no doubt to ease the tension of his stressful day, he bar-hopped with a number of employees, got blitzed, and divulged the salaries of everyone in the company. When I came back from vacation, the tension and politics were so thick, I needed a Ginsu knife to slice my way to my office.

In another incident, during the wedding of our office manager, a drunken Wally got in a fight with the best man's father. Next thing I knew, a brawl erupted. A table was overturned, glasses were smashed, and the bride was in tears. Wally not only made the mistake of getting drunk at an employee's wedding, he managed to ruin the event; I had to drag him out as he shouted obscenities.

Though it's hard to believe, Wally is only the runner-up story in the drunken dumbass awards. The grand prize goes to a senior manager for a company I worked for briefly. This buffoon took a few of his employees to a strip joint, got roaring drunk, and described his own personal fantasy: to plant a bomb in his boss's car. It cost him his job when one of the employees narced on him.

Don't ever let employees or business associates see you at your worst. If you say or do something outrageous in front of your employees while you're under the influence, they'll never forget it. Remember, every stupid thing you say or do can, and will, come back to haunt you.

47. THIS AIN'T NO CLUBHOUSE, NEITHER

Don't hire friends. When business and a dollar bill are on the line, friendships can end in an instant. There is always a strong temptation to hire close friends. You've known them for years. You can trust them, right? Maybe, but if you have to lay down the law, will a friend listen to you? Who knows? If he does, he'll probably harbor some resentment, and that's the beginning of the end of your friendship.

When I started my business I made the mistake of hiring several college friends. When I had to fire a few of them a few months later because they just plain sucked, I became King Asshole, and fifteen years later, I still haven't reconciled with them. I was stupid enough to believe that just because people were my friends, that made them talented. Naïve mistake.

Another close friendship was jeopardized a few years into my business when one of my employees, who also happened to be my college roommate and one of my closest friends, decided to leave the company and go to graduate school. I took this news hard, and unjustly questioned his loyalty. I put a strain on our friendship before finally wising up and pulling my head out of my ass. Friendships are too precious to let business screw them up.

Friends can be partners, but not employees. A good partnership is strengthened by friendship, but recognize that partnering up in business with a friend puts that friendship at risk. You have to decide if it's worth the risk.

I think that most of it boils down to character. If you know someone really well, you know whether you can really trust him or not. I knew that some of the people I was doing business with over the years were loose cannons with the morals of street pimps, but I chose to associate with them anyway. Maybe that was a blunder on my part, but if I had listened to the voice of common sense, I wouldn't be writing about all the great mistakes that I've made, this one included.

This lesson not only applies to hiring friends, but to befriending employees as well. Good managers separate office life from social life. In the early years of my career, this was difficult because I liked being friendly and especially liked making new friends. But I was naïve to believe that I could mix my business world with my social life. Over time, I learned the hard way that although I could certainly be friendly with the people who worked for me, I couldn't really be their friend. Why?

First, when your employees consider you their friend, they'll be more likely to bend the rules and take advantage of you. Not every employee takes this low road, but in my own experience, at least half of them took advantage of me in some way. It was usually small things like coming in late, leaving early, stretching a lunch hour, or extending a doctor's appointment into a half-day absence. But small things add up to a big problem sooner or later, and it's much harder to reprimand a friend than it is to chastise someone you have no emotional connection to. Employees will think twice about bending the rules if they're not sure how their bosses will react if they get caught.

Second, you can't get too emotionally attached to your employees because, through any variety of circumstances, you might have to lay them off or fire them. At times I've set myself up for true mental anguish when I had to let a friend go. I was wracked with guilt and regret, even when the circumstances that led to the termination were out of my control. It was painful, especially when the employee I was canning had a family I had come to know. At least for me, it's better to remain distant so that when bad times come (and they do, sooner or later), I don't suffer more than the person I'm firing.

Third, you might set yourself up for some serious emotional pain if a workplace friend betrays you. If it can happen to Monica Lewinsky, it can happen to anyone. Betrayal is a damned hard thing to cope with. If you don't believe me, just ask my shrink.

Still, at times I can't help but take the risk of befriending employees. Some of my best friends are people who have worked for me. But I've been burned as many times as I've made a lifelong friend, so choose your work friends wisely, especially if they report to you.

Likewise, *don't hire family members*. Even if your family members are perfect for a job, don't do it. Why risk a family feud over a job?

Keep your family and friends in one compartment of your life and your business associates in a completely separate one. Don't blend the two, or you might be the only person at your next birthday party.

48. GRILL YOUR JOB CANDIDATES

As a business owner or manager, you should always be on the lookout for new talent to recruit into your organization. Whether you're in growth mode and need to hire a number of employees or you're out to replace a single employee who has moved on, it's your responsibility to find the best candidates for the job.

Early in my career, I was a weak interviewer. I asked a few basic questions and if I got a good vibe, I made the candidate an offer. Sometimes I got lucky. A lot of times I didn't, because I didn't dig deeply enough.

Years later, when I was involved in a new start-up, it was my job to staff an entire product development team of upwards of forty people. This time, I decided to really push the envelope when it came to interviewing. I sat down and composed a list of interview questions I thought required quick thinking, introspection, communication skills, and most important, common sense. These questions helped me become a better judge of character. After a few rounds of interviewing, I could deduce pretty quickly who was genuine and who was a bullshitter. My probing interview questions were not what most people expected. A few candidates froze up and some were uncomfortable, but in general, I found that most people welcomed the opportunity to talk about themselves.

I would start every interview by introducing myself and the company. Then I would fire away. Here is my list of my questions. Maybe you can use a few of them next time you have to hire a new employee.

1. Tell me about yourself. What are your qualifications?
2. What interests you most about this job?
3. What are the skills you most want to improve at this stage of your career?
4. What job tasks do you find easiest? Hardest?
5. Are you willing to work overtime when necessary?
6. You're facing a deadline and you know you're going to be late. What do you do? Do you take the time to finish your work the way you want it, or do you make concessions to ensure the deadline?

7. How do you handle pressure?

8. Describe the most stressful, difficult problem you've faced professionally. How did the situation turn out?

9. How do you keep up on current events?

10. What was the last book or movie you really enjoyed? Why? Who is your favorite author?

11. If you were asked to work on a project you knew nothing about, how would you approach learning about the subject matter?

12. How do you organize and plan for major projects?

13. How do you accept criticism?

14. How do you take direction?

15. Tell me about a time when your work was criticized.

16. Do you enjoy dealing with the public?

17. Do you consider yourself to be a good writer? Speaker?

18. Give me an example of when you've gone the extra mile.

19. What did you like about your last job?

20. What did you dislike about your last job? (YOU CAN SURE SPOT TROUBLE FAST BY ASKING THIS ONE!)

21. How long would you stay with our company?

22. What are you most proud of—personally or professionally?

23. What are a few key lessons you've learned from the jobs you've held?

24. What have you done that shows personal initiative?

25. What do you think your references would say about you?

26. Are you able to collaborate with others?

27. Do you prefer to work with groups or by yourself?
28. Are you open to all personalities? Who can't you work with?
29. Tell me something I may not know. Some bit of trivia, an interesting fact . . . anything.
30. Tell me about an event that profoundly affected you.
31. Are you a person who sticks to strict routines, or are you flexible?
32. In your opinion, what is the essence of art, programming, writing, producing, composing, accounting, selling—or whatever the job is?
33. What do you think determines progress in a company?
34. Do you consider yourself to be persistent? Aggressive?
35. Have you managed a budget? How large was it?
36. What is your attitude toward traveling?
37. Do you think this job will bring out the best in you? Why?

Some of these questions really brought out the best—and worst—in people. I remember interviewing one person who went on and on and about how he hated his last job and boss. Strikes one, two, and three—you're out, in my book.

As I retyped this list I thought of people long forgotten and remembered some of the insightful and surprising answers that many of them gave me. I got to know a lot about the people I was hiring before they even received their first paycheck. Like Santa Claus, I knew pretty much up front who was naughty and nice.

Just be careful not to ask anything too personal while you're interviewing—marital status, children or no children, ethnic origin, religious beliefs—or you could get into big legal trouble. And don't try to get clever in an attempt to dig into someone's personal life. Don't show a picture of your children to someone and then ask if they have children of their own or ask, "Jesus Christ is my personal savior. Who's yours?" or "If you were traveling somewhere to trace your ancestry, where might that be?"

If you're the one being interviewed, be prepared for anything. If your interviewer has a Pittsburgh Pirates pennant on his wall, don't tell him that you love the Phillies, or you have no one but yourself to blame. Once I was interviewed by a guy who had pictures of Porsches all over his office walls. During the interview he asked me what kind of car I drove. I was in a jam. If I admitted to my shamelessly boring domestic sedan, I would blow the interview. But I couldn't risk being caught in a lie. I assured my interviewer that one of the big reasons I wanted the job was so I could finally buy a German sportscar. He offered to help me with the purchase. My spur-of-the-moment answer earned me points. I was offered the job (complete with a car stipend), but I turned it down, partly because I realized that I didn't want to work for anyone who would actually think less of me for driving a Pontiac.

Finally, don't be reluctant to ask people to demonstrate their skills on the spot. This is a great way to let the stars shine. Once, when I was hiring a public relations director for my company, I ended interviews by asking candidates to write a sample press release. I gave them the pertinent information and material, escorted them to a private workspace, and gave them thirty minutes to show their stuff. Some of the people who could say nothing wrong during their interviews fell flat on their faces when it came time to write.

49. SET THE BAR HIGH

Employees are a reflection of the companies they work for. Once you've hired an employee, set high standards from the outset. *Don't tolerate mediocrity.* Take the time to train new employees thoroughly and then demand that they perform to A level. If they can't cut it, don't waste time. Get rid of them and continue searching for better people. A-level talent is out there; it's just hard to find.

I can't tell you how many times I've tolerated mediocrity just so that I didn't have to deal with all of the baggage and stress associated with firing someone. I hated to hurt people's feelings. I've had to deal with a spectrum of emotions when I've had the "this just isn't working out" talk. Some people are so blinded by their egos that they argue vehemently; others break down and bawl like babies. A few people have walked out and quit; a few more have pleaded for a second chance. It was a source of stress that I didn't want to deal with, so I often let people slide. The result? My "silk glove" approach weakened my company. Mediocre people produce mediocre products, and mediocre products don't sell.

I think people either have talent and ability or they don't. If they don't, chances are they never will. Only a handful might be worth an extra effort. Follow your gut instinct to determine who is salvageable and who still couldn't do their job even if you dunked them head-first in the holy waters of Lourdes. Bite the bullet and make your cuts fast, even though it's a stressful, unpleasant chore.

In television and movies, the big shots and villains have no qualms about looking someone in the eye and saying, "You're fired." But for all of the tough talk in the wonderful world of film, seldom do you ever really hear the phrase "you're fired" in the workplace. Why? Because companies are paranoid about firing mediocre workers for fear of being sued. Instead they'll employ what they call "employee improvement plans." What a crock. A whole new plan of minitasks has to be devised, implemented, and managed so that inferior workers can take micromanaged baby steps in an attempt to learn basic job skills and common sense. It's a huge waste of time and money to set up a system in which it is nearly impossible for employees to lose their jobs. What's the upside for the extra time, effort, and cash that a company has to expend for an employee improvement plan? I don't see one. At best, mediocre employees will learn to keep their heads above water, but they'll never be very good. I'd rather take my chances searching for a new recruit than waste a nickel on a bogus improvement plan.

50. SHUT UP AND LISTEN

Learn to *listen to your employees*. Don't be the kind of manager who never shuts up, who talks over everyone in the room, who argues for the sake of argument's sake, who won't let a conversation end, who is always thinking about what to say next instead of LISTENING to what's being said in the present moment. Don't be the kind of leader who crams the most words humanly possible into the smallest idea.

Did you ever notice that the people who never shut up at the office are the same people who are in way over their heads? In an attempt to mask their insecurity about being clueless wonders, they preach, they pontificate, they babble, but they never listen. The sound of their own voices is their only comfort, their own personal meditative *Om*, their security blankets.

I'd rather work a double shift in a coal mine than attend a meeting with "blabbers." Sadly, I've worked with and for some of the world heavyweight champions of verbal masturbation. One associate I worked with a few years ago had to have the last word at all costs. And worse, her last word was always a little dig, an insult, a suggestion on how you could do your job better.

Then there was the Emperor, the delusional CEO I mentioned

in 6, "Don't Get Attention Deficit Disorder." When it came to someone who couldn't listen, the Emperor led the league. No task was too great. Nothing was impossible for his troops. He commanded his employees to perform impossible tasks, and if they raised doubts he called them quitters. When legitimate concerns were voiced, it was as if he threw a switch and his brain turned off his hearing. If only he could have removed the rocks from his ears, he could have saved himself and his business, but you could never tell the Emperor anything. He knew best, just like Napoleon did at Waterloo.

When I was a manager, I was an average-to-good listener. Though I grew weary of it, I always listened to my employees' complaints and concerns. It wasn't a fun part of the job, but it was the best way for me to take the pulse of my operation. I learned to keep my ears open around the office and pick up on the gossip and rumors.

People inherently like to talk. Use that fact to your advantage. Ask questions. Encourage your employees to speak up.

51. SHUT UP AND LOOK

Open your eyes and *observe how your employees interact with one another*. And *pay attention to how you interact with everyone you come into contact with*.

When I had my own business, I was always so knee-deep in my own world that it would take an act of God to get my attention. At a point when there were only twenty employees in my company, I was completely unaware of the scandals brewing. Two employees were having an office romance that turned ugly. The tension mounted daily, but I didn't notice a thing—until the woman started throwing things at the guy in the office. The sound of obscenities and glass smashing finally got my attention. At the same time, another employee was stalking two female employees. To top it off, a few of my animators were out of town interviewing for new jobs. With so few people to manage, I should have been aware of every dirty secret, but I was clueless. It took a crisis to erupt before I woke up and realized something was rotten in the state of Denmark. And once a situation in the workplace blows up, the damage is almost always beyond repair.

Here's another common scenario I faced: Two employees who work together hate each other. Tension intensifies. Their boss may or may not be aware of this tension, but regardless, he does nothing about the situation. Finally, the situation erupts. It becomes apparent that the company is not big enough for both of these employees. What do you do? If you say, "Make them shake hands and be friends," wake up. There are three obvious solutions, and none of them are pleasant:

a) You may have to shuffle these employees around so that they have no contact with each other. This may work, but it will undoubtedly affect your products and schedules.

b) You may, like some of the more horrific managers I've known, decide to pit the two feuding employees against each other until one devours the other and drives him out of the company. This "pitting people against each other" management strategy is becoming more and more popular because cowardly managers don't have to do their own dirty work.

c) Or you may have to make Sophie's choice by choosing which employee you like best or who does the best work, publicly siding with that employee and running the other employee out of the company.

Last year, this Sophie's choice scenario took place in the front office of the Pittsburgh Steelers football team. The tension between Bill Cowher, the head coach, and Tom Donahoe, the director of football operations, was so great that they could no longer work together. Dan Rooney, the owner of the Steelers, had to choose sides. He chose Cowher. Only time will tell if his decision was a wise one.

How can you avoid these no-win scenarios? Get nosy. Sniff out problems like the dogs that zero in on drugs at the airport. Wake up! Open your eyes! Analyze the chemistry between your employees. See who is flirting and who has the evil eye. When tension surfaces, get to the bottom of it and put a stop to it fast. Bring people together and guide their dialogue. If you're perceptive and quick to act, you'll be able to thwart little problems before they become major issues.

52. JUST SHUT UP

Don't divulge secrets, whether it be confidential information about your business or personal information that an employee may come to you with in confidence.

Tell employees only what they need to know. You may think you can trust an employee to keep a secret, but nine times out of ten, that secret will be passed along, and that's how stories get blown out of proportion. If you start sharing the wrong kinds of information, your employees will lose focus. Suddenly they'll get caught up in the daily behind-the-scenes drama instead of doing their work. In the late

1980s, a lot of companies in my industry were using a strategy whereby every employee was told everything that was going on in the company during a Friday afternoon company-wide meeting. I thought initially that the strategy was a good one, but over time, I learned that while it's great to share information when things are going well and there's money in the bank, when you start reporting financial woes or sales disappointments, productivity plummets. Panic spreads like a virus. In my opinion, it's better to keep most company-related information under wraps until it affects your workforce directly, but as soon as it does, share the news quickly and honestly (See 54, "Speak the Truth").

Remember to *be sensitive with personal information that employees may come to you with behind closed doors.* When I was a manager, employees came to me with all kinds of problems, including their marital woes, illnesses, and financial troubles. I wish I could say I kept my word and didn't divulge any of their secrets, but I let my tongue slip more than once. While I know I'm certainly not the only person who has betrayed an employee's trust, I don't like to compare myself to the managers I know who do this regularly. This is certainly one of the more shameful mistakes I've made in my career.

53. THINK FAST

Kill time and you kill your career.
—B. C. Forbes

React quickly when changes need to be made. When layoffs, firings, cutbacks, or product cancellations are the best solution to a crisis, be honest and do it fast.

When my company got into its first life-and-death crisis, there was no doubt that the first thing I needed to do was cancel a project in development and lay off the entire group working on the product (which amounted to about 30% of my workforce). It was my first major taste of failure. I worried about the employees I would be forced to cut. I dragged out the layoffs for weeks, hoping for a miracle that never occurred. In the end, the layoffs were unavoidable, but by procrastinating, I not only suffered weeks of personal stress, I continued to go into debt by covering payroll for employees who should have already been cut.

Even huge corporations make this mistake. An entertainment company I did contract work for dragged out a layoff for three months. Everyone knew of the impending cuts, and while executive management hemmed and hawed, employee morale and productivity were in the toilet. By procrastinating, you're not fooling anyone, especially your workers, who can always sense impending doom.

It's so easy to procrastinate when it comes time to making significant changes in the workplace, but don't fall into this trap. By avoiding the pain and stress associated with making the tough decisions, you'll further weaken your company.

54. SPEAK THE TRUTH

Don't employ the mushroom management technique. That's when you keep your employees in the dark and feed them bullshit. Don't lie and withhold information that has a direct impact on your employees' lives.

If you're currently working for a lousy manager, you probably never quite know what's really going on. That's how I felt when I worked for one. I was never sure if I was in line for a bonus or a pink slip.

Be honest with your employees when you have bad news to

deliver. If you have to lay off a percentage of your workforce, *tell the truth as soon as the decision is made*. When layoffs are the only option, extend your employees the courtesy of letting them know that difficult times are ahead, that their jobs may be on the line. Don't drop bombshells on them.

I've made this mistake, with two results. First, the stress associated with firing people compounded because I kept the news to myself. Second, the employees who were caught blindsided by the news never forgave me for not being truthful.

I've recently been on the receiving end of the same kind of dishonesty. A couple of years ago, I designed and wrote an adventure game for the interactive division of a well-funded high-tech company. Shortly after I completed my work and moved on, the company, despite a strong product track record, closed the entire interactive division without warning. More than 300 people were simultaneously thrust into unemployment. Little did any of us know that the company's commitment to the games business was strictly speculative. How could we have guessed? The company was hiring like mad and relocating people from hot job markets all over the country. Only after they had milked every employee did they decide to bail out of the industry. And though I was long gone by the time it happened, the closing of that division impacted me. The product I worked on for seven months was shelved when the division closed. Had I known the company was considering pulling out of the interactive business, I would never have taken the job.

You won't be fooling anyone if you try to hide the truth. People can inherently sense trouble a mile away. Don't sugarcoat bad news. Just be honest. You'll not only be doing your employees a service, you'll feel a whole lot better about yourself.

A good leader tells employees the truth, good or bad, and makes them feel as if they're part of the company's success or failure, that they're deserving members of their organizations.

55. DON'T PREACH DOOM

Employees feed off of the emotions of their superiors. Even in times of crisis, try to be positive. Maintaining an even keel keeps morale and productivity on a steady track.

Inherently negative people make the worst business leaders. I know this for a fact because I was one. Even on relatively happy days, I would see the glass as half-empty. In times of crisis, I was the King Kong of negativity, the Monet of despair, painting bleak scenarios that hung like dark clouds in the office. During bleak periods, my steady pessimism fostered a truly miserable work environment. My negativity was contagious. Every employee absorbed it, and productivity sank when I got worried.

Now that I've had some time to reflect on my years in business, I believe that things are never really as good or bad as they seem. I wish I could have just looked at situations realistically and cut out all the drama and fear.

Remember, your employees will look to you to determine the state of the business. If you want to bring the best work out of your workers, be a positive force. Even if you have to fake it, just put on a happy face.

56. KEEP PROMISES

Saying "I promise" versus "No guarantees, but I'll try" can make all the difference in your credibility. *Don't make promises to your employees.* Promises are important things. Honor is on the line. When someone makes a promise and either keeps it or breaks it, it says a lot about that person.

If you do make promises, keep them. Early in my career I handed out promises like sticks of gum. I promised employees everything from promotions to raises to extra days off, but then, for one reason or another, I was often forced to break my word. Immediately, I lost credibility and respect, and once I lost my honor, my company lost its heart and competitive edge.

These days, I never make a promise unless I can keep it. If people ask me to promise something that I may or may not be able to deliver on, I tell them I'll do my best, that's all. That keeps my conscience clear and doesn't put my credibility at risk. Some people may accuse me of being noncommittal, but I think that's better than being called a liar.

57. MAKE UP YOUR MIND ALREADY

Be willing to make decisions. That's the most important quality in a good leader. Don't fall victim to what I call the "Ready-Aim-Aim-Aim-Aim Syndrome." You must be willing to fire.
—T. Boone Pickens

There is no more miserable human being than one in whom nothing is habitual but indecision.
—William James

I don't know about you, but I'm sick of so-called business leaders who can't even decide whether to have Coke or Pepsi at a company birthday party, let alone make decisions regarding human lives. Time and money get flushed when executives drag out their decisions, even the most trivial ones. If you truly want to be a breath of fresh air in the business world, be the kind of leader who isn't afraid to make decisions.

People in positions of power hesitate to pull the trigger on decisions because by doing so, they put their necks on the chopping block. If the decision turns out to be a good one, they can bask in the glory and take the credit. If the decision is bad, they're in trouble. Only after a decision is made does the sweating begin. That's why people waffle back and forth on viewpoints, debate endlessly, and run from decisions.

It seems to me that the "to decide or not to decide" conundrum is a bigger problem now than it was five years ago. In the early days of the computer games industry, product decisions weren't labored over like they are now. Now, the big movie studios have interactive game divisions that are investing huge sums developing games that sometimes don't have official "green lights" until they are nearly finished. This strategy may serve the movie industry, where a few million dollars lost on a movie that's shelved is no big deal, but computer games aren't movies. Most games don't gross even one-tenth of what a movie does. Companies that I've done contract work for have cancelled projects so late in development that they've literally lost millions because someone at the top lacked the testicular fortitude to make a decision up front and stick to it. All the people banding together to create the games—the artists, programmers, designers, writers, and audio designers—are dragged out, never knowing if their work will ever actually be seen and played by the public. And in an industry where credits on published titles open doors, this is an impossible way of life.

Decision-making isn't hard if you're not a coward. When it's time to make a decision, look at all the facts, sketch out all of the possible scenarios, analyze them from all angles, formulate a plan, and pull the trigger. Your decisiveness will win you respect. And what's the worst thing that can happen? You "screw the pooch," as the

Mercury astronauts used to say. Big deal? It's not the end of the world. Learn how to cover your tracks and become a political animal and you'll weather the storm. We'll get into that more in chapter 4, "In the Trenches."

58. TELL THEM WHAT YOU WANT

Judge others by clearly defined criteria. If you're like legendary sports agent Mark McCormack, yours might be leadership, attention to detail, and follow-up. Mine might be completely different. Whatever the criteria, make sure that all of your employees know up front what is expected of them. *Be specific.* Don't change the rules once they've been set.

Managerial dictators constantly change the rules. A good leader—and how few of those there are in the world—defines the rules of the company or a project up front and then sticks to them. Last year, a company in my industry decided to develop a product line for a new product genre. A friend of mine was hired to head up this new division, but halfway through the development of the first product, the CEO of the company changed his mind and pulled the plug. My friend was unemployed before her furniture arrived from the cross-country move.

Always let people know exactly what is expected of them, how they will be evaluated, and what you won't tolerate as their manager. *Be clear.* Leave no room for misinterpretation.

I was often far too vague when it came to laying down the law. I wanted to be liked, to be everybody's buddy, so I adopted a flexible approach. Sure, there were rules, but I let people bend them. And when certain employees started getting away with murder, the other ones lined up to follow their lead. That's how I often lost control.

If and when I manage again, I would gather my employees

together on my first day and let them know exactly what pisses me off, large and small. I would be sure to cover the basics, things like skimming an extra half-hour at lunch or showing up late or leaving early. Next, I would get into more specific, project-related rules and regulations. Not only would this approach clarify my position as project leader, it would make people think twice before they attempted to take advantage of me or break the rules. Sure, they might poke fun at me and call me a tyrant, but so what? The ground rules would be set, and whether you're tough or a pushover, your employees will still make fun of you, so you might as well be firm. You're not out to win a popularity contest. If your job is to manage others, then clear communication is a must. Just stick to your performance criteria, and when the first person decides to bend your rules, come down on him like you're unleashing the wrath of God.

59. DON'T CRITICIZE A JOB WELL DONE—PRAISE IT

A pat on the back is only a few vertebrae removed from a kick in the pants, but is miles ahead in results.
—Ella Wheeler Wilcox

Appreciation is a wonderful thing; it makes what is excellent in others belong to us as well.
—Voltaire

When employees do a good job, praise them, don't criticize them. Early in my career an angry employee told me that I was never happy with his work, that I made him feel bad about himself. What a crock! I thought he was great, and I argued the point.

"But you never tell me that," the employee said.

He was right. I never complimented employees on their work. Though I wanted everyone to praise me, I never saw fit to praise others. That was the day I realized that everyone needs a pat on the back for a job well done.

I had made a mistake, but it was an innocent one. Withholding praise was not a premeditated tactic on my part. A more serious mistake is when negative feedback is employed as a motivational tactic, even in positive times. When an employee shines for his company, many managers, fearing their praise may inflates egos and dull the competitive edge, will say something like, "You did okay, but I know you'll do better next time."

Negative feedback does nothing but build resentment, which leads to frustration, anger, and hatred. Employees are made to feel worthless; nothing they do is ever good enough. At a corporate outing last year, I played golf with a human resources director from a Fortune 500 company, and he confirmed that the "negative feedback" management style is encouraged in their "corporate culture" (one of my favorite buzzwords!).

Managerial dictators also throw tantrums and dress down their employees in open forums just so that no one forgets how big, bad, and important they are. Many so-called cutting-edge managers who are featured regularly in the business trades are notorious for belittling their employees. The head of one of Hollywood's major studios should, according to most people who have been on the receiving end of his immature tirades, carry a rattle and a pacifier with him to meetings.

While I didn't purposely use negative feedback in my daily approach, I was far from being a positive motivator. After my employee showed me the error of my ways, I vowed to change. I began handing out compliments like Monday morning doughnuts. I was as in a hurry to make up for lost time as Scrooge on Christmas morning. It didn't take long before this strategy backfired on me. Because I was praising everyone—even when their work wasn't praiseworthy—my compliments carried no weight.

When I got a fresh start in a new management position a few years later, I resolved to compliment only great work, and to be reserved with my praise so that when I gave it, it meant something. This strategy worked well for me.

Stick up for your employees. Demand that others outside the company show respect to your employees. Don't let your workers be doormats for other companies you work with. When outside people walk all over your employees or badmouth them, stick up for your people, and they'll stand by you.

Regularly honor and reward excellent performance. *Buy business cards for each and every one of your employees.* They only cost twenty bucks a box, and I guarantee you, it will be the best money you ever spend. There's a sense of pride that comes with handing someone your business card. Employees will feel like they belong.

Incentives like *employee of the month and year awards* may seem hokey, but they've worked for me, especially when cash bonuses were tied to them. It doesn't have to be thousands of dollars; a couple of hundred bucks means a lot to many people. So does a trophy or plaque. Rewards go over well as long as they're presented sincerely.

One of my boyhood idols was the late Willie Stargell, the power-hitting captain of the Pittsburgh Pirates. In 1979, Stargell started handing out what he called "Stargell Stars" to players on the team for excellence on the playing field. They were little adhesive gold stars that the players affixed to their caps. Stargell's little gesture sparked the team's morale. The Pirates, who weren't expected to have a .500 season, went on to win the World Series. By the end of the season, the players' caps were covered with gold stars. Here were grown men, most of them wealthy beyond their dreams, playing like kids again, exceeding their abilities, just to see who could end the season with the most gold stars. Everyone in Pittsburgh was hooked, me included. I cut gold stars out of felt and glued them on my cap. I sat around dreaming that Willie Stargell would come to my house and give me a star for a wiffle-ball home run or an "A" on a class essay.

Be creative. Know what motivates your employees. Perhaps an employee loves to eat at a certain restaurant or is a die-hard fan of a particular sports team. Reward him or her with a gift certificate or a box seat ticket to a game. But remember, make people earn the rewards. In the words of James Boswell: *He who praises everybody, praises nobody.*

60. DON'T JUDGE PEOPLE BY THE TIME THEY LEAVE

Your business should have a required eight-hour day. Even though your work hours are defined, *respect the fact that everyone has different work habits.* Some employees may get into the office at 7:00 A.M. and leave at the stroke of five. Compare that to another employee who may come in at 8:30 A.M. on the button, take a half-hour to get settled, bullshit with other workers for half the day, and then leave at 6:30 P.M. You're actually getting more work out of the early bird than you are from the person who looks as if he's putting in overtime.

One manager I knew judged people by the time they left in the evening. It didn't matter that some employees came in at the crack of dawn and got quality work done while the office was deserted and quiet and then left at five. He didn't respect the fact that some employees simply couldn't stay past five because they had to pick up children from day care. One employee, with whom I still work today, was always on his blacklist for leaving at five despite the fact that she was probably our most efficient employee. She came in, did prolific amounts of work speedily, and was always on schedule. She didn't work late or on weekends because she didn't have to. But he always questioned her commitment and loyalty because she wouldn't live in the office; eventually he gave her the boot because she wouldn't change her lifestyle to please him.

This manager's favored employees were usually the young guys who were single and had nothing better to do than stay in the office around the clock. Because he had no social life, he was right there with them. At night, the office was like a frat house, with music blaring and takeout food everywhere. When I walked the halls, the sounds of gunfire and carnage coming from Doom death-matches were deafening. For every three hours of overtime those brown-nosing frat boys logged, less than an hour of productive work was accomplished.

This kind of "kudos for voluntary overtime" mentality is prevalent everywhere. At night, you'll see lights on in offices all over town, but how many of those people are really working? Too bad business owners are too naïve to realize that a lot of these candle-burners are doing nothing more than surfing the net, downloading porn, playing games, working on freelance projects, talking on the phone, and conducting job searches on their company's dime.

If a business is being managed properly, no one should have to work unreasonable hours. *Don't judge employees by the time they put in at the office. Judge them on the quality of work they perform while they are there.* Don't be fooled by the time sheet.

By the same token, beware of so-called "flex hours." At one company I worked for, employees could work five extra hours from Monday through Thursday and then take Friday afternoon off. Almost everyone took Friday afternoon off, but less than half of the employees were putting in the required five hours earlier in the week. Since no one in the company was tasked with policing the situation, it became an honor system. Need I say more?

Unless you have a hardass baby-sitter in place to monitor everyone's schedules, I advise against instituting any form of flex-time program.

61. HAVE A PLAN TO KEEP 'EM

When you've built a stable of talented employees, you have to do everything in your power to keep them. That means dealing with compensation issues fairly while being careful to not overpay your talent.

When I owned my own business, I avoided having a defined policy for salary increases. I was afraid that I might be forced to award raises at a time when the company was having cash-flow problems (which was almost every month).

Raises were awarded only when the company had some money in the bank (usually after a new product had shipped). The entire compensation issue was at my discretion. Sometimes well over a year would pass before the subject of raises was even discussed. When employees pressed me for a raise, I would blow them off, change the conversation, and utter something like, "We'll be looking into that issue soon."

This nebulous approach to employee compensation not only dragged down employee morale, it cast a bold spotlight on the fact that our company wasn't a serious or stable one. By trying to protect the company and myself first, I showed my employees no respect, and I lost a number of talented people. Looking back now, I would never have worked for someone like myself, someone who didn't give a rat's ass about his employees' careers.

If I started a new company today, one of the first things I would do would be to institute a yearly employee review process that took place at the same time every year (the time when cash flow is expected to be at its peak or when your calendar or fiscal year has just ended). This review process would be the sole determining factor for employee salary increases and the granting of employee bonuses and stock options (if applicable).

My review process would work like this:

1. Define the Career Track

Some people go to work and never know where they stand in the corporate hierarchy, nor do they have any idea where they'd eventually like to wind up.

First, managers should clearly define the job tracks for a particular position. For example, a production assistant needs to understand that his career track would look something like this:

1. Production Assistant
2. Assistant Producer
3. Associate Producer
4. Producer

5. Senior Producer

6. Director of Development

7. Vice President of Development

The entire promotion ladder should be laid out for employees so that they never have to second-guess where they currently stand in the organization and where they might eventually rise. If a production assistant has aspirations to be a programmer, artist, or writer, his manager should take his goals into consideration and move him to a new career track if and when the time is appropriate.

A defined career track allows employees to enjoy a greater sense of accomplishment as they climb the company ladder. And, of course, each new job title should have its own compensation scale.

2. Set Yearly Goals

Next, employees should sit down with their managers and define what their yearly objectives are up front. Financial targets and project responsibilities should be the main area of focus. Since companies are often forced to make substantial changes in strategy during the year, flexibility should be built into this process. The main purpose of this task is to get defined objectives on paper so employees know up front what is expected of them. If an employee is struggling with some kind of problem area, these objectives might focus exclusively on the improvement of those weaknesses. Be as specific as possible. If rules are defined up front, employees will have no excuses if they don't measure up.

3. Have a Thorough Review Process

Once a year, managers should review their employees' progress. This detailed review might be broken into specific areas such as:

a) An analysis of whether the employee failed to meet, met, or exceeded yearly objectives.

b) An analysis of the employee's accountabilities and responsibilities.

c) A review of the employee's present job skills. How much has an employee improved or learned during the year?

d) How well did the employee work with others on team projects?

e) How well did the employee communicate, in written and verbal form?

f) What leadership characteristics did the employee demonstrate, if any?

g) How did the employee demonstrate initiative? How did the employee solve problems? Did the employee act without always having to be told to?

h) Did the employee have a positive attitude?

Managers, as well as employees, should fill out a detailed yearly report in which all of these issues are detailed. For each major area— for example, leadership, communication, collaboration, yearly objectives, and so on—managers should determine if employees are performing exceptionally, satisfactorily, or poorly.

Poor employees should get a written and verbal warning to improve, with the threat of possible termination. They should receive no more than a cost-of-living adjustment. Satisfactory employees might receive a 3 to 5 percent raise at their manager's discretion. Exceptional employees could be eligible for a 5 to 8 percent increase.

Employees should be able to read these reviews and comment. But whether they agree, disagree, bitch, or moan, in the end, the manager makes the call.

The review process should be a major yearly event for managers and employees. Managers who blow off the review process or don't give it their best effort shouldn't be managers for long.

I recommend that the topic of raises be addressed only during the review process. If an employee comes to her manager in the middle of the year and demands a raise, the answer should be NO. If, however, an exceptional employee comes to you and tells you she has another offer, you may have to award a raise on the spot if you want to keep that person. Just make sure you see your star employee's competitive offer *in writing* before you dole out the salary increase.

4. Make Employees Earn Promotions

Promotions should be awarded only when the company has a need for someone to fill a new job position. When it comes time to promote an employee, tell employees that in order to get the promotion they seek, they have to prove they can do the job first. In other words, have them do the new job for a set period (probably 90 days) at their present salary. This saves money and protects the organization from people who decide they can relax and coast after a major promotion.

62. HAVE A PLAN TO CAN 'EM

While it's critical to have a clearly defined plan to keep your best employees, a plan that lets you get rid of your worst ones is of equal importance.

Years ago, I was sued by an employee I had fired. Because I didn't have a dismissal policy, he won a hefty judgment against my company. While my mistake was that I didn't have a dismissal policy of any kind, many large companies have the opposite problem. They have defined dismissal policies that are so complex that employees practically have to strut around the office naked to get fired. Many megacorporations with thousands of employees will purposely carry deadweight because they're afraid that ex-employees will retaliate with discrimination and wrongful termination lawsuits. Rather than risk a lawsuit, companies shuffle mediocre talent from division to division, department to department, instead of doing the logical thing—FIRING THEM!

When it comes time to define your dismissal policy, start by instituting a 60- or 90-day probation period that allows you to terminate new employees for any reason. You'll need that little red button that safely allows you to eject loose cannons.

After your employees survive the probation period, they should be given a company handbook that details a clear dismissal policy. I've found that a dismissal policy works best when an employee can be fired after one written warning. Some companies require one verbal warning followed by two written warnings, but that's overkill. Poor employees who deserve to be fired shouldn't be given the opportunity to walk a tightrope of mediocrity just so they can avoid their next warning. Don't specifically define the offenses for which a warning can be issued. Be vague so that you can issue a warning for both work-related and behavioral offenses. Do, however, define definite causes for immediate dismissal—things like fighting at work, insubordination (directly disobeying a superior's reasonable instructions), drugs or weapons possession on the premises, breach of the nondisclosure/noncompete agreement, or revealing privileged financial data such as his/her salary, other employees' salaries, or revenue/expense data. If someone wigs out in the office, you want to be able to boot them on the spot, so be as specific as you can when describing grounds for immediate termination. As always, be sure to consult your corporate attorney when defining these policies.

Don't be afraid to cut deadweight. If employees threaten to sue you, let them. As long as you have just cause for terminating them and you follow your dismissal policy, you have nothing to worry about.

J. Edgar Hoover, the notorious FBI director, was famous for collecting dirt on anyone and everyone and then tucking it all away in his personal files. Managers should definitely have a little Hoover in them. Build a strong file on problem employees before you send them packing. Document poor performance and bad behavior and tuck it away until the day you need it.

63. SQUASH THE SNAKES EARLY

Trust your instincts and get rid of troublemakers as soon as they rear their ugly heads. There are two kinds of troublemakers in the workplace. The first kind of troublemaker is the harmless fool. These are the pains in the ass who gripe, complain, and make waves. Everyone in the company knows that harmless fools are jackasses who aren't to be taken seriously. They pose no serious threat because no one, from top to bottom, has respect for them. If you have a harmless fool working for you and you don't need him, cut him loose. You'll be doing everyone in the company a favor. If, however, a harmless fool is a critical member of your team, learn to ignore him.

The second kind of troublemaker, the snake, is a far more dangerous creature. Snakes are the troublemakers who actually have talent and political savvy. As a manager, you have to learn to recognize the snakes that slither in your midst. If you're managing one of these creatures, watch your back, because most likely he or she is after your job. Snakes will stop at nothing to get what they want. They'll knock on your office door bearing gifts and, with warm smiles, praise you as they size up your office and decide what color to have the walls painted.

In 76, "Beware of the Snakes," I share some methods of snake detection. But here's the first one: When you're not sure if someone is a snake, start a conversation with a reptilian suspect and raise non-work-related issues, especially subject matter that should elicit some kind of emotional reaction. To demonstrate true emotion, one must possess a soul, and snakes, being utterly false and empty beings, will trip all over themselves when something besides corporate conquest is being discussed. This little trick works like garlic on vampires. You'll know if you have a snake on your hands within five minutes.

I tried this technique on a suspected snake I'll call Soulless Joe Jackson. When I was returning to the office after lunch, I saw a little kid chasing his dog down the sidewalk. The dog did a sudden U-turn right into traffic and—BAM!—kept on running straight down the road to canine glory! Back at the office, I pretty much ruined everyone's day by telling the sad tale during our team meeting. There were only two dry eyes in the room, both belonging to Soulless Joe. He sat there clutching his spreadsheet while everyone else reminisced about their beloved pets.

Once you've pinpointed a snake, sharpen your blade, wield it, and don't let your conscience get in the way. Find a way to discredit snakes before they discover a path leading over your head. Make their work lives miserable. If you're lucky, maybe they'll give up and quit, but if they're persistent, you'll have to find grounds to fire them. Issue them warnings. Use your rank and position. Remember, snakes are out to kill you, so bite back. If you turn a blind eye, snakes will slither into the minds of your other employees. Once their influence grows, you're in big trouble.

I learned this lesson from working with a King Cobra a few years ago. There were at least three instances on which I had legal grounds to fire this reptile. He continually bad-mouthed the CEO in front of other employees; he encouraged employees to interview with other companies; and he harassed several of the women in the office. I had more than enough ammunition to pull the trigger on his career, but I left him off the hook. Why? Because I was too damned nice. Believe me, there were no rewards for showing this corporate snake mercy, at least not in this life. As soon as I had a fallout with the CEO, King Cobra was the first person in line to betray me. Not firing him when I had the chance is a mistake that still haunts me. If I caught a leprechaun right now, you can guess what one of my three wishes would be.

You need a killer instinct when it comes to snakes. They're like ants in your house—they have to go. I'm a pretty nice guy; I meditate, once in a while I even burn incense, but if I find ants in my kitchen, I spray them with Raid and enjoy doing it. They really annoy me. That's the way you have to be with corporate scoundrels. If you don't kill them, they'll find a way, sooner or later, to kill you.

64. IF THEY DON'T WANT TO BE THERE, GET 'EM THE HELL OUT

No doubt there's a lazy bum wasting space in your workplace. Every office in the world has at least one. These are the "I don't give a damn about my job and I wish they would just lay me off so I can collect unemployment" types who moan about everything, show up late, leave early, and frequently suffer from a mystery virus that prevents them from showing up at work. They're also the people who will never quit of their own volition. They'll hang on as long as they can until someone finally gives them a golden ticket to the unemployment office.

If you're stuck managing losers who don't want to be there, get rid of them and quit wasting good money. Chronic whining is a contagious disease. Before you know it, whiners can poison the minds of those around them. Being subjected to constant pessimism can drain the life out of even the most vital person. If you don't believe me, just ask my wife what it's like to be married to me.

A few years ago, a producer I'll call Daisy Lazy hired me to write a design document for a game. After my first week, it was clear that Daisy just plain hated the very concept of work. When I reminded her that she was smack in the middle of L.A., where there are more jobs than palm trees, and that she should find a job that made her happier, she dismissed the notion. She confided in me that she was shooting for the bum's lucky lotto: the layoff, the severance package, the yearlong government gravy train. She used to come in in the morning and pray that she'd be the first name atop the long-rumored layoff list. Unbelievably, she survived two layoffs while I worked with her on the project. While talented and ambitious people were herded out of the office like cattle on the way to the abattoir, Daisy Lazy survived like a cockroach after a nuclear blast, mainly because the project she was working on was high-profile and critical for fiscal year projections.

On the project we worked on together, Daisy hired a creative writer (I'll call him F. Scott Fitzjackass) who was truly the poster boy for this lesson. During his contract negotiation, F. Scott demanded, and got, a significant "kill fee" so that if the project was cancelled at any point during his tenure, he would receive the total contract amount. Before the ink was even dry on his contract, F. Scott was sabotaging the project, complaining, whining, and refusing to work. He did everything in his power to wreck the project. It was fun to watch his pathetic efforts fail. Like Freddy Krueger, the project wouldn't die. After months of politicking, protesting, and not writing a single coherent sentence, F. Scott was forced to dash off a script in less than two weeks. I've read better writing on Cheerios boxes.

Life is too short to beat your head off a wall in frustration while you try to appease losers. I dented my share of walls until I finally learned to *cut the deadweight*. There are a lot of people looking for jobs who are smart, talented, and eager to work. Go the extra mile to find them.

65. YOU'RE NOT ARCHIE BUNKER

I am free from all prejudice. I hate everyone equally.
—W. C. Fields

If you're a business owner or a manager, *don't be stupid enough to discriminate.* Here in the twenty-first century, this should be a no-brainer, but for a lot of amoral human beings, it's not. Bottom line: Always hire the best people for the job, or you'll be courting serious legal problems.

The president of one of the companies I worked for was a world-class racist, a borderline skinhead. During one layoff, he ordered me to let ten people go (out of about 50 employees). The layoffs weren't unjustified; the company was too fat for its own good. What was unjustified was the fact that he used the so-called layoff as an opportunity to drive out everyone who didn't fit into his male-dominated, Aryanesque vision, including all of the homosexuals and African-Americans we employed. I was on my way out of that company and I knew it, so I wanted to nail that scumbag to the wall. I hoped for a lawsuit. I wanted a lawyer to ask me under oath if I had ever heard the owner of the business use the word "dyke." I wanted to nod my head and say, "You bet I did. And here's the list of dates and times I heard him say it."

None of the terminated employees took action, despite urgings. They could have banded together for a devastating class-action lawsuit, but their major concern at the time was to find work.

I've also had to deal with sexual harassment issues. Once, a painfully shy employee timidly knocked on my office door in tears. Her boss had done something to offend her, and she was visibly shaken. For an hour, I tried to get to the bottom of her complaint, but she couldn't bring herself to tell me what happened. I tried to reason with her: "How can I take action on your behalf if you won't tell me what happened?"

She hesitated, then broke down in tears. Jesus, did this guy assault her? Finally she spilled the beans. Apparently the suspect in question pinched the woman's midsection and informed her she had to lose some "puddin'." Certainly not the worst offense imaginable, but an offense nevertheless.

This manager was on my blacklist already. I wanted to fire him, but the woman didn't want to feel responsible for her boss's termination, so she asked me to move her to another team. I showed the manager mercy, issuing him a warning for verbal harassment and touching an employee inappropriately.

Race and sex are only a few targets for corporate bigots. There are many others. One of my friends, who was an upper-echelon manager for a dot-com company, was interviewing candidates for the director of quality assurance position. The best candidate for the job was a competent, talented woman who happened to be obese. When my friend informed her superior, the senior vice president of the division, that she wanted to hire this woman, the VP told her of one of his major hiring philosophies—evaluating candidates based on what kind of company they would make when traveling with him. The woman was passed over for the job even though she was, without a doubt, the best candidate.

66. BEWARE OF THE LEECHES

If an employee wants an advance on his pay or a loan from the company, don't give it to him. It sets a bad precedent, and before you know it, everyone will be lining up for pay advances.

You'll be shocked and surprised to learn that many people borrow money from friends, relatives, and coworkers without any intention of paying them back. I've made the mistake of personally lending $600 to one of my employees. This was the same lummox who, a few months later, was fired for sleeping on the job. I've never seen a nickel of repayment. If he doesn't pay me this year, I finally plan to take a charitable deduction.

In the future, if someone asks me for a loan and my gut instincts tell me that the person is trustworthy, I will offer to go to a bank and co-sign as a guarantor for the loan, and make the person make the monthly payments. That would put responsibility for the loan in the person's hands and commit him to a fixed repayment schedule. This strategy would, more than likely, weed out the losers looking for a free handout. Give it a try next time someone hits you up for a loan. If the person has honor, he won't balk at your plan.

67. MANAGERS ARE CARD-CARRYING MEMBERS OF THE BABY-SITTERS CLUB

One of the truly underrated talents of good managers is their ability to listen to all of the whining, fretting, and backstabbing and cope with it without committing some kind of criminal assault. Compensation issues, personality conflicts, "He said this," "She did that"—managers must change 100 poopy diapers a day.

You're either the kind of manager who doesn't mind being a parent or the kind who can't stand kids. If you truly enjoy absorbing yourself in other people's lives, God bless you. You'll go far in the business world. But if you're cranky and intolerant like me, you'll either have to learn to accept the fact that human beings are imperfect or move to a cave in the thin air of the Himalayas.

Good managers are not only bosses, they're baby-sitters, siblings, and psychotherapists. Employees have come to me with problem after problem, professional and personal. I've had employees ask me for tax advice, stock market tips, spiritual guidance, and marital counseling. Employees have broken down in my office and told me, in detail, how their spouses no longer felt sexually attracted to them. I've been thrust into the midst of highly personal issues like divorce, spousal abuse, and mental illness. Though I always felt uncomfortable (after all, I had my own laundry list of problems to deal with, and I am the center of the universe, after all), I had to listen, show compassion, and give the best (though cautious) advice I could. Baby-sitting was a big part of my job. Even when ridiculous issues crossed my desk, I had to handle them calmly and resist the overwhelming urge to rip people's silly heads out of their asses.

How silly did it get? I once had to reprimand a programmer for continually replying "Your momma . . ." to every question that someone asked him:

"Fred, did you get the new animation added to the demo?"

"Your momma added it last night."

"Fred, do you want to go to lunch?"

"Your momma wants lunch" (usually accompanied by some kind of obscene gesture).

Fred had to be suffering from some kind of bizarre psychological malady, probably something in the Tourette syndrome family. He spewed obscenities around the clock. Some of the other employees began to feed off of, and build upon, the foundation of profanity he had laid. Soon the office sounded like a locker room. I had to issue a written memo warning a number of employees to stop the profanity or else. Fred responded by inventing a swear word code list. One stood for *shit*, 2 for *ass*. I'll let you fill in the rest. If I recall correctly, there were some thirty-plus codes on his complex spreadsheet, which was distributed to his inner circle. Soon, I was hearing things like, "Yeah, well you're a two, three, eighteen, twenty-one." After a day or two of that nonsense, I had to issue final warnings because the employees were spending more time memorizing their swear word codes than working.

Another time, a human resources director for a company I was working for visited our branch office to distribute the new company handbook. After work, he ended up taking several employees out to a strip club. An HR director taking employees to a sex club isn't the worst part. He actually handed out company money to employees so they could pay for lap dances. Guess who was tasked with busting his chops about it?

My favorites are the employees who shed tears for their laid-off comrades, then fifteen minutes later ask me if they can have a fallen coworker's ergonomic keyboard. They're like vultures. Have some respect for the dead!

But the Baby-sitter of the Decade trophy goes to one of my former bosses. The company employed more than 300 people. Over a period of several weeks, women were arriving at work in the morning to find an alarming little present waiting for them: Someone or something was sneaking into the office in the dead of night and defecating in the sinks of several women's restrooms. The Mad Crapper, as he became known, had the code to enter the building, so all employees were immediate suspects. But since the volume of these fecal surprises was immense, the eye of suspicion fell on the men. Over the next two weeks, the Mad Crapper struck no fewer than five more times.

Finally, my boss called a company meeting to address the problem. He held a plunger aloft and uttered a single unforgettable phrase: "This shit has to stop—NOW!"

A hidden camera finally caught the culprit. The Mad Crapper turned out to be a 400-pound employee who was most widely known for two things: unabashedly removing his shirt every summer during the company picnic and chewing on open sores that blistered his arms and hands. Why he chose such a grimy method to punish women is still a mystery. I only thank my personal God I'm not his psychotherapist.

Talk about giving your manager shit! My boss not only had to devise a plan to catch the culprit, he then had to actually fire the loon.

Just remember, part of every manager's job is dealing with employees' personal issues. That's life. Grit your teeth and bear it. And when you can't take it anymore, remember, there are a lot of vacant caves in the Himalayas.

4

IN THE TRENCHES

Sometimes in politics, one must duel with skunks, but no one should be fool enough to allow the skunks to choose the weapons.

—Joe Cannon

This section may seem a little too *Art of War* for the innocent, but I've been scarred by office politics, so I speak from experience. Work environments are not always nice places; in fact, many of them are miserable. I think a lot of businesses are like big, bubbling cauldrons of soup: The people at the bottom get scalded while all the scum rises to the top.

I'm not going to preach goodwill and tell you that if you smile and play fair, your positive energy will rub off on your bosses and coworkers and your workplace will become a haven of joy. If you believe that, I have some autographed sports memorabilia to sell you on E-bay. Office politics stink, but if you turn your back on them completely, you'll get stabbed. You have to be smart enough to know when and when not to fight back.

I've heard many people say, "Business is a game." I disagree. Games have consistent rules that make the playing field fair and level. In business, there are no rules. Every company is different.

If business isn't a game, what is it? It's a combination of war and theater. You play a part in an ongoing soap opera full of complex characters and changing plots that unfold on a battlefield instead of a stage. To succeed and advance, you have to possess the political savvy to know when and how to be boastful or humble, loud or quiet, kind or ruthless, compassionate or vicious.

While you're out to succeed, other people are out to get you. Chances are, if you're sitting pretty in your organization, someone very near you has it out for you this very moment. Maybe he just doesn't like you. Maybe he's after your job. Perhaps you threaten him. Sooner or later, though, if you don't play smart, you'll lose.

There have been times when I did the fighting and times when I was slaughtered. I've spent fifteen years in the bloody trenches of office warfare, as both a participant and an observer. Here are some of mistakes made and lessons learned.

68. DON'T TAKE IT PERSONALLY

Money and power corrupt. It's a tale as old as time. Julius Caesar was stabbed in the back by Brutus. Christ was betrayed by one of his own disciples. Steve Jobs got booted out of the company he co-founded. Business is a nasty black cauldron full of bitter ingredients—suspicion, lust, anger, hatred, doubt, fear, greed, and betrayal.

The only good thing about the whole ugly mess is that *politics in the workplace are seldom personal.* Most plots launched against you will not be orchestrated because your work is not good or you're a terrible person. Most corporate politics are driven by desires that have tempted mankind for ages—money, status, and power. Somebody wants your job title; someone wants your salary. When riches and power are on the line, don't be surprised by any act of betrayal. *In business, expect to get the shaft.*

In the workplace, events often play out like a professional

wrestling storyline. One guy waits until his so-called friend turns his back and then—WHAM!—he clobbers his partner over the head with a chair just so he can get his shot at the gold belt.

That great line from *Chinatown* comes to mind. Crusty old Noah Cross, the soulless, power-mad tycoon with a lust for power and a passion for incest, looks Jake Gittes in the eye and says, "You see, Mr. Gittes, most people never have to face the fact that at the right time and the right place, they're capable of anything." Ain't it the truth?

I don't handle betrayal well, even the kind of backstabbing I can see coming a mile away, but the next time I'm in a position to be betrayed, I'll prepare myself, professionally and psychologically. I'll have eyes in the back of my head. I won't hold out an ounce of faith that people will do the right thing.

How will I do that? I'll share my secrets in this section, but for now, just remember—*don't take any of it personally.*

69. SELL YOUR SOUL OR OWN YOUR LIFE

When you climb to the highest levels of an organization, the company will most likely want your soul. *Be prepared either to give blood freely or to turn down promotions that will create conflicts in your personal life.*

Don't believe the myth that you can easily balance your life when you have a one-dimensional boss who lacks a life outside the office and expects you to also give up your life for the sake of the business.

At many companies, when you get that big promotion and raise, get ready to burn the midnight oil. Have to pick up your kids at day care or take them to the doctor's office or a Little League game? "Tough shit," your boss will say, or at least think to himself after you leave.

Will a new promotion require a lot of travel? How about weekend hours? If so, start kissing your weekends good-bye and pack your suitcase, because you'll probably be living in hotels.

I'm certainly not encouraging people to turn down big promotions. Just realize that everything has a price. If your family means the world to you, know what will be expected of you before you accept a higher position. If weekend camping is your passion, make sure you're not expected to camp in your office every Saturday and Sunday night.

Be honest with yourself. Can you live with the inevitable sacrifices you'll be expected to make when you climb the ladder? If so, start handing out those new business cards. If not, stay where you are.

70. EVEN THE DON CAN GET WHACKED

Never be so vain and arrogant to believe that your company can't survive without you. *Always be prepared to be chopped.* Everyone is expendable, especially executives and employees who are paid handsomely.

A few years ago I did contract work for a company that was preparing to initiate a large layoff. An employee I was working with was unconcerned. "They know I'm too valuable to cut," she told me.

A few weeks later, she was first on the chopping block in what became a corporate bloodbath. She was utterly stunned. "Are they insane?" she asked me.

"Of course they are," I told her. She didn't realize that in times of crisis, there is no justice or fair play. The decision-makers aren't in their right minds. It's like a monthlong full moon. When layoffs become unavoidable, executives panic and do two things. First, they do everything they can to protect themselves so they can keep their jobs and maintain their salaries. A paranoid, insecure executive will cut twenty smaller salaries just to preserve his own inflated one. Second, executives under the gun act too fast for their own good. What should be major business decisions are simply impulse reactions based on quick glances at red and black numbers on a spreadsheet. Reason and logic are tossed out the window. Decision-makers are too stressed to take into account personal histories and past performances.

Actually, a friend inspired me to write about this topic. Though she's a vice president at a major company, she's been around the block enough times to know that the ax can fall at any second. She always has her files and personal effects within reach so that if she gets whacked, she can be free and clear of her office in less than ten minutes.

71. BE LIKE SPOCK

If you want your career to live long and prosper, be like Mr. Spock. He didn't do cartwheels when Shatner saved the day. Nor did he panic when the Klingons were firing torpedoes and the *Enterprise*'s shields were down. Spock just went about his business and kept his emotions at an even, steady keel.

Who knew what was really going on in Spock's brain? Maybe those smartass slights from Bones McCoy got Spock's Vulcan blood boiling. Spock might have had all kinds of emotions churning inside him, but he never showed them.

Act without emotion in business situations. Pray to the Vulcan gods if you have to, but learn to keep your cool.

For years, I wore my emotions on my sleeve. You would never have to wonder if something was bothering me. I've been so angry

I've broken out in hives; I've brooded and sulked when I was spurned. And every time I let my emotions show, I handed my adversaries ammunition with which to shoot me. I also let stress manifest in my body. At different times in my career I've suffered from many classic self-induced maladies, including stomach pain, rashes, insomnia, and depression—deep, dark, ugly depression.

It took me eleven years to realize that the business world I was living in wasn't the most important thing in my life. Now I've learned to take business-related matters with a grain of salt. Once in a while, something will happen to spark my anger, but it's rare.

It's no one's business what's really going on inside your head, and it's far more advantageous to act with an air of mystery than to be an open book that everyone can read.

When someone slights you, let it roll off. In a few weeks, the scab will heal. Counter personal attacks with calmness. Be firm and factual. Don't give anyone, least of all your enemies, the satisfaction of knowing that they got to you. Meet a negative approach positively, and you'll make your enemies squirm.

Practice verbal aikido: when someone insults you, take that attack and cleverly redirect that negative energy back on the attacker. How? Ask questions. If you really want to drive your attackers crazy, ask them questions and demand specific answers. If you refuse to hurl insults back and calmly ask question after question, you'll plant an amazingly fruitful seed of doubt in their minds and rock their illusory worlds. Reacting calmly will also make you look better in front of an audience if your rival attacks you in public.

Wear a poker face. In 17, "Zip Your Lip," I wrote about a former boss's spectacular poker face. During negotiations he had the look of a mental patient who had just undergone a lobotomy; when he wore that vacant look, he was nearly impossible to read.

Learn to act instead of passively react or overreact. Don't fly off the handle, or you may shoot yourself in the foot by saying stupid things.

I love the *Godfather* movies (except for the third one, of course). I especially admire Michael Corleone's emotional balance in *Godfather II*. When someone tried to threaten Michael, he remained calm and cool and always wore his poker face. When he played one side against the other, he remained a mystery.

That's how to act in business. *Capisce?* Michael Corleone's face was never flushed with anger. He never lost his cool. That was Michael's brother, Sonny. And look what happened to him.

72. LET THE CRITICS SPEAK

Learn to listen to criticism without stressing out, blowing your top, or pouting. You, me, everyone—from the president to the pope—is criticized and will be until we retire. Everyone's a critic. Insecure people always want to make themselves feel important by bashing other people's work. If you let people's nitpicking get under your skin, you'll be worm's meat long before you'll be cashing out your IRA. Don't fight criticism; accept it as part of work life.

It's not easy. Criticism has been a hard thing for me to cope with. For nearly a decade, I had total say over my projects. People could make suggestions freely, but I had the power to toss their ideas aside. Once I began freelancing, I found myself in a whole new world. Everyone from the CEO to the soda machine stock boy suddenly had a say in my game designs. My stomach churned; I developed TMJ syndrome (no kidding). In order to get paid, I not only had to listen to criticism, I had to swallow it whole, and it made me sick.

If I ignored criticism, however, I would be labeled a prima donna and my career as a freelancer would go up in a mushroom cloud. If I listened to criticism—most of which was a joke—I would drive myself crazy. After much introspection and good old-fashioned therapy, I've come to accept criticism as simply part of the job.

It took a couple of years, but I've changed; criticism no longer drives me over the edge like it used to. Some criticism has even been useful. A few ideas and suggestions will be good; most will be disastrously wrong. I incorporate good suggestions and fight bad ones. I don't always win my arguments, but at least I'm not afraid to voice my disagreement.

Bottom line: If you balk at criticism, no one will want to work with you. *If you accept criticism without serious emotional scarring, you'll be a sane, well-employed person.*

73. TOOT YOUR OWN HORN

If you want respect and appreciation, *remember to sing your own praises when you accomplish one of your milestones or go above and beyond the call of duty.* For years, I resisted tooting my own horn because I thought it made me look arrogant. After all, no one could forget the fine work I had done in the past, right? Wrong! How soon they all forget.

Despite a steady track record and professional work ethic, there have been many times when my work has gone unappreciated. That's no one's fault but my own. I've learned that people who never let others forget about the good work they do are the people who survive and thrive in cutthroat business environments.

If you're in charge and things are going smoothly, your superiors may believe that your job is too easy. They may not realize that you're busting your butt, managing myriad daily tasks, and putting out dozens of minifires to keep your projects on track. It's sad, but woe-fully true.

Business is anything but fair. You might have accomplished a thousand miraculous tasks that fattened your company's bottom line, but don't expect your bosses and colleagues to raise you up on a pedestal. People have short and very selective memories. It's a "what have you done for me lately" world we work in.

Look at the ruthless world of professional sports. Babe Ruth was arguably the greatest baseball player ever. The Babe singlehandedly filled Yankee Stadium for years. He was the heart and soul of our national pastime. But the minute his bat cooled off, the Yankees released him. Can you imagine letting Babe Ruth go? If an injustice like that can occur, why should the business world that you and I work in be any different?

It's up to you, and you alone, to keep the memories of your past successes alive in the minds of your bosses. No one else is going to do it for you. Don't be obnoxious in your approach. Just let your superiors know that you're getting the job done. Your bosses would probably have no qualms about telling you off if you did something wrong. Why not tell them when you do something right?

If you feel as if you're being mistreated, demand a meeting and remind your bosses of your past accomplishments. Don't let your good deeds be forgotten. Use E-mail. Speak up at company meetings, but walk the fine line between humility and egotism cautiously. If you come off like you're the Second Coming of Christ, that your company could never survive without you, you'll be pegged as a loudmouth instead of a team player.

Experiment with the volume of your horn. Toot it a few times and see what happens. If you come on too strong, you'll know.

Adapt, change your approach, turn it down a notch, and you'll find your proper volume.

Tooting your own horn allows you to plant a seed in the minds of your bosses, a seed that serves as a reminder of your competence and contribution to the company. Once that seed is planted, fertilize and water it on a consistent basis.

I've survived a number of corporate layoffs, both as a participant and an observer, and I've noticed that there's always at least one naive employee who believes that he is untouchable because the executives in charge truly recognize his talent and worth. These are the employees who, when ousted, are shell-shocked and outraged by the injustice of it all. In business, don't expect justice or fair play. "Fair business" is a contradictory term, kind of like a celibate hooker. You have to create your own justice, and you do that by standing on your soapbox and letting everyone in the company, especially your bosses, know that you are valuable. *Those who toot their own horns the loudest are often the survivors in times of crisis.* So start tooting, and toot often!

But . . .

74. KNOW WHEN TO COOL YOUR JETS

As a manager, I always felt like kicking myself when I was dumb enough to hire someone who didn't know how to play it cool during his first few weeks on the job. You know the kind of person I'm talking about—a new employee who comes out of the gate like a pit bull with a bursting bladder. Instead of easing into his work environment with grace and dignity, he arrives on the scene and pisses all over everyone and everything in the company in a pathetic attempt to mark his territory.

I remember hiring one kid—whom I'll call Johnny Rah-Rah—fresh out of art school. He was young, eager, talented, energetic . . . and too obnoxious for his own good. During Johnny's first week on the job, he openly critiqued his coworkers' art and offered to help them improve. He also stepped on his boss's toes by suggesting that new procedures (taken directly from his academic textbook) be adopted in the art department. His criticism extended beyond his own department. He criticized the programmers, writers, and game testers, unabashedly stating his philosophy that everyone had room to improve. The tension bubbled; it seemed only a matter of days before someone strangled him.

Johnny pounded the final nails in his coffin when he asked me for a raise before his probation period was over and then criticized me for not using enough contractions in my memos. I had warned him several times to tone down his act, but he just didn't get it. It was my pleasure to send him packing.

People like Johnny don't grasp a simple business fundamental: You can't get ahead by pissing everyone off, especially the boss. *All it takes is a little savvy and common sense to know what to say, when to say it, and how to say it to make your mark without making enemies.* If you lack these basic skills, learn them fast, or you'll be unemployable.

75. TRUST NO ONE

Be friendly and fair with everyone, but don't expect loyalty in return. Business and friendships don't mix. I've been burned dozens of times for letting my guard down in front of employees and coworkers and paid a steep price for letting my work world bleed into my real world (See 47, "This Ain't No Clubhouse, Neither").

I'm not suggesting you pull your head into a turtle shell and become the next Ted Kaczynski. Be friendly, laugh, joke, smile—but *don't show your cards and don't trust anyone!* Be cautious . . . and suspicious. When more money, a better title, and a bigger office are on the line, people will change their colors faster than a good guy in a professional wrestling storyline. People in whom I had total faith have betrayed me, and it created a lot of wounds that are still healing.

A few years ago, I made the mistake of butting heads with the owner of the company I was working for. Talk about digging a hole for myself. I soon found myself in his doghouse, and the funny thing about it was that no one had to tell me I was living with the pooches. It became obvious that the owner was bad-mouthing me to everyone because people I had worked with for years started to treat me differently. It felt like *Invasion of the Body Snatchers.* One day I went to work and everyone emerged from pods to do me in. My so-called friends started cutting me out of meetings. The lunch invitations stopped. The after-hours socializing ended.

But even after being treated like a leper by almost everyone in the office, I didn't regret my defiance. Nor did I resent my co-workers who opted to choose the side of the guy signing their paychecks. That was the smart (and only) move for all of them to make. What I do regret is trusting a few of them more than I should have. And I doubly regret going to bat for a lot of the people who ended up stabbing me in the back.

Don't fall on your sword for anyone at work. Before you risk your job by sticking up for a coworker, ask yourself, "Would this person do the same thing for me?" We all have our own struggles to fight in the workplace. Don't make yours worse by carrying everyone else's burdens along with your own.

Cold as it sounds, I'll never make the mistake of trusting people again. As far as I'm concerned, everyone is out to screw me. If people turn out to be loyal, I'll be pleasantly surprised.

76. BEWARE OF THE SNAKES

There isn't a work environment in the world that doesn't have at least one troublemaker roaming the halls. *Keep your eyes and ears open, because there's always a Machiavellian scoundrel in your midst,* a villain who wants what you have.

Pay attention and know early who the backstabbers and gossip hounds are and be careful what you say and do around them. Recognize the snakes—the people who don't like you, who are out for your job, who consider you a threat. Never distance yourself from anyone, including the snakes. Better to interact with your enemies than to cut yourself off from them. When you remain distant, you send a clear message that you're on to them; that's when snakes often become the most venomous.

Treat your snakes like friends. Smile, laugh, joke, pretend that everything a snake says is brilliant, interesting, witty, and insightful. Let snakes believe they're your friend. Just don't give them any real ammunition to use against you. *Never share or divulge personal information to snakes.*

Learn to read people. See 63, "Squash the Snakes Early" for advice on how to pinpoint a snake. Here are a few other warning signs that help you determine if a coworker slithers:

- Has the person in question ever gone behind your back by setting up a meeting with your boss without your knowledge?
- Has this person complained about you to others?
- Has this person upstaged you or tried to make you look bad?

- Has this person tried to bait you into saying negative things? When you speak to them, do they talk as if they're wearing a wire? (Who knows, they might be.)

If you answered yes to any of these questions, get the snakebite kit ready. The person in question is probably a reptilian scoundrel. Proceed with extreme caution.

The mistake I've often repeated was to not bite back when a snake tried to bite me. I used to think that no boss with a brain in his head would ever take a snake seriously, but I was wrong. A lot of insecure executives rely on snakes to tell them exactly what they want to hear.

Trust me: If a snake bares his fangs, fight back. Most snakes are too anxious for their own good; they get careless and strike too fast. If you're smarter, more subtle, more confident—if you have a more pleasing personality—you'll win the fight.

If a snake goes behind your back, don't stand for it. Look him in the eye and say, "I know what you did and I don't like it." If a snake bad-mouths you, tell him, "I know what you said about me. Do you want to say it while I'm standing here?" Most snakes will stammer and deny they said anything. That's because behind the venomous fangs of most snakes lies an insecure coward afraid of confrontation. The more fearless you are, the less chance there is that a snake will try to bite you again. Go toe to toe with total certainty that you're right and the snake is wrong, and you'll defang your serpentine enemies before they ever have a chance to inflict damage.

77. CHECK YOUR TONGUE AT THE DOOR

A big mouth can end a brilliant career. Be careful what you say, and especially who you say it to. Your words can and will come back to haunt you if you're not careful. Think about the people who are on the brink of disaster in your own organization; chances are, they're the ones with careless tongues.

Sometimes a big mouth can work to your advantage (See 73, "Toot Your Own Horn"). But a big mouth is like a loaded pistol. When used properly, there's no better weapon. When used carelessly, you can accidentally do yourself in.

1. Be careful when you talk behind someone's back

I'm not going to lie and say I never bad-mouth others. Sometimes, when anger is sparking, I just can't stop myself. But over the years I've learned that bad-mouthing others has serious potential repercussions.

One of my coworkers—a guy I'll call Denny Deathbytongue—made an epic mistake when, over happy hour drinks, he openly bitched about the president of our company in front of me and three other employees, including the office secretary. Unbeknownst to Denny, the secretary was the president's sister-in-law. I gestured for him to shut up, but he ignored me and kept ranting. A week later, he was unemployed.

Analyze the situation before you put your mouth in overdrive. Be smart. Ask yourself these questions:

a) Is the person you're complaining to trustworthy? (Hint: the answer is always no, unless they're your mother—and you know you can trust your mother)

b) Is the person you're complaining about at your same level, or could he or she potentially fire you?

c) Will the person you're talking to run and tell the person you're complaining about? If so, is your gripe easy to explain away, or will you have to face an ugly confrontation that you may not be in a position to win?

When someone bad-mouths you and you get wind of it, try to use it to your advantage. An ex-boss made a stupid mistake when he bad-mouthed me in front of several employees at the company picnic. A loyal informer shared the news with me later that night. Several others confirmed the report. I knew at that moment that it was time for me to leave. I took advantage of the fact that my boss couldn't keep his big mouth shut. I knew that he lacked the courage to have it out with me face-to-face or to fire me, so I rode it out for a few months and planned out the next phase of my career.

2. Don't be two-faced

Being two-faced can lead to a tragic downfall of Shakespearean magnitude. If you bad-mouth someone, have the guts to tell him to his face if and when he confronts you. If you get caught in a lie, you can kiss your credibility good-bye because you'll be pegged as a coward.

3. Don't play the gossip game

A little gossip is a fun diversion from the daily grind, but don't be the center of your office's gossip mill. Why risk your credibility by fueling rumors? Let the idiots do that. Sooner or later, gossip hounds piss off the wrong person. Don't be standing there chatting with them when their big mouths finally do them in.

4. Don't share your personal problems with your peers or your boss

Employees have come to me with personal problems and secrets, and I've betrayed them by telling others (See 52, "Just Shut Up"). I'm not proud of it, but I've done it, and I don't even consider myself a bad person. Think about it: How many family members and close friends have blabbed your personal secrets? Those are the people who love you, for God's sake. Imagine what some of the scumbags you're working with will do. You might as well broadcast your personal life over the airwaves.

78. WATCH THE PLAYING FIELD

Pretend you're a general overlooking the battlefield that is your workplace. Consider each person and *analyze your alliances*. Know who can help you get where you want to go and who has the power to thwart you.

Business has its seasons and cycles. Pay attention and always know who the golden child of the hour is and who is on the boss's blacklist. Don't just possess this information, use it to your advantage.

When I fell out of grace with one of my bosses, I advised a coworker who was a close friend to betray me by siding with him over me. I was planning to resign within weeks, but for my friend, his so-called betrayal elevated him within the organization, where he remained for several years after my departure.

Be smart. Don't go toe to toe with coworkers who are higher on the totem pole or with employees who, even though they're at your level, have more clout. Never start a conflict unless you're sure you can win.

Know whose ass is worth kissing. Don't be an obvious brown-noser, but get to know the people who matter. Find out what makes them tick, and give them a reason to remember you. I climbed pretty high in one organization because I'm a good golfer. When the owner of the company took up the game, I invited him to play a round. He took me up on the offer, and we ended up playing regularly. I was the only person in the company who had the boss's ear for four or five hours at a pop every week. Don't worry, though—I didn't stoop so low as to let him win.

79. DO THE WRITE THING

The written word is your greatest form of protection in the workplace. *Get everything in writing. Put everything in writing.* Constantly follow up with letters, memos, and E-mails.

Don't trust anyone's word. The CEO of a company I worked for promised me my yearly salary as a bonus if he was successful in raising a new round of venture capital. I didn't ask for the promise in writing because I didn't want to adopt an adversarial position that would make me look suspicious. A year later, after the financing deal was in place, my boss suddenly developed amnesia. All I had was a verbal promise that proved to be as worthless as an impotent porn star. I lost out on a five-figure bonus because I was stupid enough to believe my boss was indebted to me morally instead of legally. Don't make the same mistake. Demand that all oral agreements be presented in writing. Who cares if you offend a fragile ego? Tell your boss that it's not personal, it's just a safety measure because you've been burned in the past. Crack a joke. Tell them that if Saint Peter promised you a spot in the heavenly choir of angels, you'd ask for it in writing. Do whatever you have to do to smooth over tension, but *get that piece of paper!* And if your boss won't give it to you, then you'll have gained some priceless insight into the person you're working for.

Personally, I have a lot of respect for people who don't trust me. They're playing it smart. Once an employee demanded that I give her written confirmation regarding a compensation issue. I wasn't offended in the least. I wrote out a detailed memo that outlined the issue to her satisfaction. Thanks to that memo, she collected a far healthier severance package when her division closed than her fellow employees who took the company's word at face value.

Detail everything you say and do. You'll especially want to document all conversations and agreements if you're in a position to evaluate others. If you are well armed with dated facts and present those facts with utter certainty, you will win the battle nearly every time. This leads to my next topic . . .

80. BE WELL-ARMED WITH FACTS

Write down everything you say and do at work. Buy a blank journal and begin filling it. Document all meetings, telephone conversations, and oral agreements. Save pertinent E-mails. *Be a very specific, detail-oriented archivist.*

Since the day I began my career, I've kept a business journal. My written accounts of meetings have bailed me out of many a mess. I've witnessed a number of my peers get burned because they were too disorganized and unfocused to keep a written account of their daily business dealings. Right now, if you asked me who I met with on April 1, 1987, I could tear the tape off of a big box of journals in my garage and produce a fairly detailed account of that day.

Most people lack the patience and focus to cover their bases by documenting facts. Why? Because it's a tedious chore to write down notes from every meeting, log phone calls, and save E-mails. But when it's your word against someone else's, being well armed with dated facts gives you a distinct advantage. While your opponent is trying to recall who said what on what date, you can volley facts and quotes like tennis balls. That's when all of the tedious information collecting pays off.

In 1990, a subcontractor sued my company, and the case went before the National Arbitration Association in Washington, D.C. We were in the midst of a crippling cash-flow crisis and I didn't have money to blow on lawyers, so I defended the case myself. My opponent went all out, hiring so-called "expert" consultants to appear on his behalf. But despite his legal team and umpteen experts, he couldn't find his ass when it came time to produce specific meeting dates and conversations. My opponent took the stand and, as I expected, his testimony was a disorganized mess. I did my homework well and was armed with figures, dates, and quotes.

I won the case, mainly because this ass-clown not only blackmailed me, he did it in writing. When I produced the letter in which he threatened to quit halfway through the project unless I paid him more money—in cash—I felt like Perry Mason. But even if I couldn't have produced a smoking gun, I still would have won the case because I had detailed written accounts of our meetings and he didn't.

81. GET PISSED OFF

Earlier I wrote that politics in the workplace are seldom personal. *Seldom* is the key word in this sentence. There may be times when you find yourself on the receiving end of an *ad hominem* bureaucratic attack strictly because someone doesn't like you, is threatened by you, or is out to climb directly over you. I've witnessed it and I've lived it, and it's not fun. If it happens to you, don't take it lying down.

I also wrote earlier that in business, you chould expect to get the shaft. I never said, however, that you had to accept the shaft silently. When people use you as their own personal toilet bowl, get mad and let them know it. If you don't voice serious displeasure the first time a purely personal attack is launched against you, you'll become a permanent doormat in your workplace.

I've made this mistake time and again. I've allowed partners, business associates, and employees to wipe their boots on me. Why? First, I'm just too damned nice for my own good. I've never been tough enough. I wish that I didn't care whether people loved or hated me, but I do. I want to be liked, even by total strangers who wake me up on a Saturday morning to sell me magazines over the phone.

Second, I'm terribly passive-aggressive. When someone screws me over, I get to brood and complain about the world and its wicked ways. At some subconscious level, I welcome abuse. That way, I'll always have a fresh supply of firewood for the flames of my self-created misery.

Last, I'm too trusting. I thought the business associates I let walk all over me six or seven years ago would be my friends for life. Now I can't even remember most of their names.

After being violated more times than a prison inmate, I'm finally learning to speak up and voice my displeasure. I remind myself that in five years, most of the faces I'm doing business with today will become faded memories. It really doesn't matter if they like me or think I'm the world's biggest ass. All that matters is that we be able to do business in the present moment and not screw each other.

Certainty and directness intimidate even the toughest bullies. Most people who would make you their doormat are not as tough as they act. Almost everyone—bullies included—is afraid of conflict. If you face your attackers calmly and firmly, most of them will back down without a fight. Try it. If the bully backs down, your self-esteem will soar; you'll also draw an important line in the sand that your business associates know they can't cross. And if you're dealing with the rare bully who won't back down, at least he'll think twice before trying to screw you over again.

82. DON'T BE A PAWN

I've made the mistake of making important business decisions on a whim, even issues regarding the lives and careers of employees. I've shuffled employees from team to team, project to project, and location to location like pieces on a game board.

It's sad but true—in corporate decision-making, little thought is given to the human element; people become numbers on a spread-sheet.

Don't allow yourself to become a mindless pawn in the chess game that is corporate restructuring. If you're being transferred or moved to another project and the move is to your advantage, then go. If you believe you are needed where you already are, fight to stay where you think you belong. *Voice your opinion;* after all, it's only your happiness and well-being on the line. Don't blindly surrender your life to executives and consultants who know nothing about you or your contribution to your company.

My older brother worked for a company for more than

twenty-five years. In 1980, he was transferred from one state to another to work for a new division of the business. He accepted the transfer and began a new life. Twenty years later, the same company decided to close down my brother's division and relocate most of the employees—my brother included—back to the company's headquarters, where my brother originally started. Faced with selling his house and reluctantly returning to a place he had left behind long ago, my brother resigned from the company. Over a hundred employees accepted the transfer and uprooted their lives and families. His instincts couldn't have been sharper. Less than a year later, more than 90 percent of the relocated employees were laid off.

Another woman I worked with was transferred from Los Angeles to New York. She accepted the transfer because she was promised a raise and a new job title. Within eight weeks she fell victim to downsizing and was unemployed in a city that she never wanted to move to in the first place.

Never believe that the people playing with your life have all the answers. *When it comes to your life and your career, only you know best.*

83. BE SPECIFIC IN YOUR DEMANDS AND VAGUE IN YOUR THREATS

Sooner or later, everyone gets screwed. *When you feel like you're getting the royal shaft, when your blood is bubbling like molten lava, bite your tongue.* Don't make crazy and senseless threats, or you'll look like a fool. Instead, be specific in your demands and vague in your threats.

In my younger, more foolish days, I would threaten underhanded business associates with lawsuits, letter-writing campaigns, and calls to the press, but my wild threats did nothing but make me look like a hotheaded amateur. When I learned to play it cool and say things like, "By X (date and time), I want Y, or I'll be forced to take action that I don't want to have to take," I began to be taken more seriously.

The first key point to remember is to be very specific about what you want. If you want a report, a promise in writing, financial data, or monies owed to you, then spell it out. Leave no margin for interpretation. The second key factor is to say when exactly when you want it, down to the hour.

The final factor is to be nebulous when delivering your caveat. Don't threaten lawsuits, physical violence, or acts of vandalism. Say something like, "I'll be forced to take serious action that I don't want to have to take." That sounds more alarming to me than if you said, "or else I'll sue you blind." By being calm, cool, yet forceful, you'll be far more intimidating.

Try a little experiment the next time someone really pisses you off. When you get bad service anywhere—at a retail outlet, a fast-food joint, a hotel, an airport check-in counter—the next time someone gets rude or steps out of line an inch—don't scream and make threats. Simply and calmly ask the person for the district manager's name and telephone number. Next, ask the person for his name. Have him spell it and repeat it. Act with a cool air of confidence and power, as if you possess the power to snatch his very job if you so desire. Then watch him flinch. He'll begin second-guessing himself and fearing that he might have just pissed off the wrong person. Nine times out of ten, you'll get an apology, if nothing else. I've gotten everything from free lunch to room upgrades.

84. KNOW WHEN TO CUT YOUR LOSSES

Some of us think hanging on makes us strong, but sometimes it is in letting go.

—Herman Hesse

There are battles in life and in the workplace that you just can't win. Maybe you're on your boss's blacklist. Perhaps you're clashing with a fellow employee who turns out to be the boss's nephew. Whenever you find yourself in an impossible situation, you may have to cut your losses and move on.

A few years ago, I butted heads with the owner of the company I was working for, mainly because I wouldn't become his briefcase-carrying yes-man. As soon as the inciting incident occurred, I knew my goose was cooked. You don't throw salt in the eyes of the guy signing the paychecks and survive. There was more than a year left on my contract, and I offered to resign as long as I was paid the remainder of the contract amount. He declined. I was determined to ride out the contract so that I got what was rightfully coming to me.

So began the worst year of my career. Slowly and steadily, my boss began to stick it to me by going behind my back to the people I was managing. Though I was never officially demoted, much of my authority was stripped. Soon I was cut out of the loop. Changes were made, without my knowledge, to products I had designed. Employees I had worked with for years stopped communicating with me. Several of the best people in the company were fired because they were loyal to me.

I stayed there and swallowed all their abuse because I was stubborn. I was determined not to quit. That's what they wanted, and dammit, I wasn't going to make it easy for them or walk away from money I had earned. Plus, it wasn't all about money. I didn't want to be forced to relocate. I had a house, family, and friends where I was. I hoped the trouble would blow over and work itself out, but it didn't.

I retaliated as best I could. I got into the heads of some of the employees and dragged them into the war. I went on job interviews all over the country on company time. The whole soap opera was a joke, and I was as wrong as they were. Looking back, I should have left the minute trouble erupted. Even after I left, I still had to sue them because my ex-boss tried to stop payment on my final check. I could have made a similar salary anywhere. All staying led to was a lot of anger, hatred, dissension, and resentment. It was the most stressful year of my life, and I could have avoided that stress by doing one simple thing—cutting my losses.

Don't stay in an environment you hate. It takes a terrible toll on your physical and emotional well-being. No amount of money is worth that. Walk away. Get out with your dignity and sanity intact. The only person who likes a change is a wet baby, but change is sometimes inevitable, so don't fight it.

85. OFFICE ROMANCE . . . DANGER, WILL ROBINSON! DANGER!

This section is for all of the office sinners out there embroiled in dangerous love (and lust) affairs with their coworkers.

Some companies forbid office romance, but that's laughable. If you stick a male and a female gorilla in a pit at the zoo, something's going to happen. Why should it be any different for human beings in the workplace?

It's no mystery why the workplace is a hotbed for all sorts of sexual shenanigans. People who work closely together spend a majority of their daily lives in close proximity to one another. Plus, you always appear to be a more wonderful person to your coworkers because they see only your good side, not the dark, bitter self that lives behind closed doors.

Some of the greatest sexual fantasies of my life have starred myself, of course, and various female business associates and coworkers. Fantasies are one thing, but actually acting on them is where the trouble begins. If you're skating on the thin ice of an office romance, be careful. Relationships are tough enough, but mix work and love in the same bowl and you're tossing one hell of a messy salad. How do I know, you ask? Because I've been at the bottom of that salad bowl. My wife and I met at work. We started as coworkers, then business gave way to friendship, which gave way to some of the aforementioned shenanigans, which gave way to dating, which gave way to our engagement. What made this romance even more difficult was our decision to keep it a secret from our coworkers. Our reasoning was that it was no one's business what we did with our personal lives. For over a year and a half, we kept our relationship a secret from the other thirty people at work, and that's a tough thing to do in a small suburban town where everyone knows everyone else's business. We went to great lengths to avoid each other at work. When she came to my house, she hid her car in my garage. When I went to her apartment, I parked blocks away. We went on dates a couple of towns away. I'm sure that some people suspected; a few people even asked, but we always denied it. Trying to maintain a secret of that magnitude in a small work environment was tough, but exciting. We were always looking over our shoulders in movie theaters and restaurants. It was as stressful as it was fun. Finally, when we got engaged, we went public.

I'm certainly not going to advise you to not date your coworkers, unless, that is, you're already married. If you're single, your future husband or wife might be sitting in the cubicle right next to you. I would advise, however, that *if you are involved in a relationship with someone at work, be honest about it. Don't hide it.* All of the secrecy adds too much stress to the relationship and makes it too easy to get caught in a lie. Come clean from the start.

Realize that like everything else in life, an office romance has serious ramifications. If your boss doesn't like it or if you've violated company policy, you could be demoted, transferred, or even fired. If you're willing to take the risk, go for it.

86. KEEP IT IN YOUR PANTS

Sexual harassment is a scarlet letter you must never wear in your workplace. Whenever you make unwelcome advances, whenever you get touchy-feely, whenever you tell off-color stories, you open yourself up to a sexual harassment complaint.

Peter Principle, the worst manager I've ever seen, was done in by libido. Though he was married with children, he made unwelcome advances toward one of his employees as well as to outside business associates. In 34, "You're Not Stalin," you can read about Peter's abusive and dictatorial management style. When his employees finally cracked, they lodged a formal complaint. The employee Peter sexually harassed claimed that Peter promised to promote her if she gave in to his advances. Was it true? He said no; she said yes. Coupled with complaints about Peter's irrational and violent outbursts, her sexual harassment complaint was taken seriously. When the other business associate Peter had an affair with was contacted, she confirmed that Peter had openly harassed her as well. Less than a day later, he was escorted from the building without warning.

I've witnessed other disturbing harassment incidents. A quality assurance director I worked with always tried to massage the neck and shoulders of women in the office. Ignoring two warnings, this closet masseur was eventually canned. Another executive asked out nearly every woman in the office. When they declined, he would then badger them for the telephone numbers of their single friends. There was also an incident where a powerful executive fooled around with one of his interns and nearly lost his job over it. I've never actually met him because I was never invited to the White House.

If your work record is tarnished by a sexual harassment incident, you become virtually unemployable. What answer are you going to make up when you're asked the common question, "Why did you leave your last job?"

It's a small world full of tight-knit industries. Don't blow your career over something as stupid as trying to get laid.

87. HOW TO GET YOUR CRAZY BOSS FIRED

In 62, "Have a Plan to Can 'Em," I advised managers to collect dirt on their employees so that if they have to fire someone, they will have just cause. Well, I didn't forget you poor employees out there. *If you're working for an inept, abusive, clueless boss, it's time to start collecting your own dirt.*

While it's true that the sexual harassment complaints were the deciding factor in Peter Principle's termination, the actual complaint that launched the entire investigation was not lodged by either of the women involved, but by another member of Peter's team. This employee wrote a detailed complaint that described several incidents in which Peter lost his cool and made what could be construed as threatening remarks to the team. The employee included specific dates, times, and quotes in his memo. Instead of butting heads with his boss, this employee played it cool, kept a record of everything stupid Peter said or did, waited patiently until Peter made one stupid move too many, and then made his move. I learned a lot as I watched this whole Machiavellian drama unfold.

What did I learn? First, it's better to poison your enemies slowly than to go straight for the jugular. If you try to battle your boss, you'll lose unless you're well armed with supporting evidence. Start by documenting every stupid thing your boss says or does. Leave no stone unturned.

Second, be patient. Getting your boss fired is all about timing. Put up with his abuse until you have everything in place to take him out. Let events unfold naturally, and always keep your eyes and ears open. Don't try to bait your boss into traps. If your boss is an idiot like Peter Principle, he won't need any help digging his own grave.

Third, keep it under your hat. Play it smart. Don't let any of your coworkers know what you're doing.

Fourth, gauge the reaction of the other people working for your boss. Are they having problems with him, or is the problem strictly your own? Are other people as fed up as you are? You should act on behalf of your entire team only if you can enlist their full support. When it's time to draft a memo to Human Resources that details your complaint, word it carefully and have your fellow team members sign it with you. The more support you have, the stronger your case will be.

Last, realize that when you submit your complaint to human resources, you begin a game of Russian Roulette. It becomes you versus your big bad boss. The office won't be big enough for both of you. If your boss is deeply rooted in the company, you might be the one looking for a new job, even though every word of your complaint is true. Analyze the stakes carefully before you act. What do you have to lose? To gain? If you're comfortable with risk, let the war begin.

88. IF YOU GET SCREWED, MAKE A STATEMENT

There's always a chance your boss will screw you over for no good reason. Maybe you threaten him; maybe you went to an Ivy League school and he went to community college; maybe you're loved and she's despised; maybe you drive a Mercedes and he drives a Ford Festiva. Whatever the case, you might find yourself on the receiving end of a purely personal *ad hominem* attack. It happens all the time.

If you're lucky enough to have a sane, well-adjusted boss, you can still get screwed in a sweeping layoff. You might think you're a priceless asset to your company, that they would never be foolish enough to cut you loose, but think again. The consultants hired to make the decisions don't know you from Adam. You're just another body in a cubicle, another salary to chop. Don't expect fair play, justice, or even common sense (See 101, "Quit Bitching: Life Isn't Fair").

If you get the shaft, you can always do one important thing to preserve your sanity and dignity: MAKE A STATEMENT! Do something that people will be talking about years from now. Like what? you ask. Here are some of my favorites:

Attention, Everyone . . .

A friend of mine was fired from the company we worked at together for a lot of bogus political reasons. After she got the news, she went straight to the intercom system and broadcast to the entire building, "Attention, everyone . . . this is your now former coworker. I've just been whacked. If anybody has the guts to look me in the eye as I'm heading out the door, I could sure use a hand loading up my car." A lot of people came to her aid, but not the scum who played a part in the hatchet job. They hid like the cowards they were, and everyone recognized it.

A Warm Towel, Sir?

Despite his obvious talent and contribution to his company, an animator I know was the victim of a poorly planned layoff. I guess there weren't enough people laid off with a last name beginning with "J," because his layoff was utterly senseless. Though he was stunned by his firing, he didn't lose his sense of humor. On the Monday morning after the Friday layoff, he showed up at work with hand towels, cologne, and a tip basket and set up shop in the men's room near the executive wing. He knew he was in the one place that not even the president could avoid. For three hours he badgered upper managers who came in to relieve themselves. By the afternoon, security had chased him away, but his folk tale is still right up there with Paul Bunyan.

"Basic Complexity"

Another guy I used to work with was clashing regularly with his miserable boss, the king of buzzwords. He peppered his speeches with all the hot phrases *du jour*, including "convergence of media," "promoting vessels of change," "maximizing the upside," and "killer app."

This person wanted to leave some kind of mark before he was fired, something that would live on long after he was gone. He created a ludicrous new buzzword just to see if his boss would use it.

"Basic complexity," he explained to his boss, was a hot term being bandied about at several cutting-edge software companies to describe a fundamental design principle: computer interfaces should look basic and simple, but behind the simplicity should lie a hidden complexity. At the next company meeting, his boss used the phrase "basic complexity" nine times, and five years later, he's still saying it.

A Fashion Statement

Ten years ago, while I was attending the Consumer Electronics Show in Las Vegas, a disgruntled scribe for a computer game magazine walked the convention floor wearing a T-shirt that said (on the front and back): "*Computer Play* magazine is a fraud. They refuse to pay me for my work."

Whenever he stopped to rest, he sat in a folding chair directly in front of the magazine's booth.

Making a statement may seem vengeful or immature, but I think it's necessary for your long-term mental health. You'll remain alive in the memories of the people who screwed you, and you may even haunt their dreams. Sure, it's silly, but you'll have the last laugh.

5

LET'S GET PERSONAL

Things may come to those who wait, but only the things left by those who hustle.
—Abraham Lincoln

Not much has changed since junior high. The good-looking people are still popular, except now, instead of getting homecoming crowns, they're getting company cars and stock options.

What you look like, how you dress, where you live, what kind of car you drive, how you talk, and how you behave are still the main criteria that strangers use to judge you. Beautiful, charming people are one up on the rest of us before the game even begins. Good speakers also climb the ladder faster.

I'm not saying that you have to be on *People*'s 50 most beautiful people list, but I am saying that you must have a pleasing personality, look neat and professional, and be able to read, write, and speak well to get anywhere in life.

Here are some tips for how to look, act, and behave in the workplace, based on my own observations and mistakes.

89. IF YOU DON'T KNOW STUFF, LEARN IT

If you want to increase your value in the workplace, invest the time and money to acquire the skills you lack. Read, learn new software programs, take continuing education courses, absorb your industry's trade journals and magazines, stay on top of every new advancement. Resolve to devote a healthy portion of your free time to getting better at what you do for a living. It's not a pointless waste of energy or cash. Every dollar you spend beefing up your job skills will come back to you a hundredfold if you stay committed. Continually learning and improving not only enhances your career, it strengthens your résumé for future opportunities.

I should take my own advice. For some unknown subconscious reason, I fight technology even though I'm in a technology-driven business. I'm still using Windows 98 as I write this.

90. LEARN TO TALK RIGHT

Clear, concise, confident verbal communication is a business must. I'm continually amazed by the poor communication used by top-level managers working for some of the biggest entertainment companies in the world. Here are some of my verbal pet peeves:

1. Don't forget to LISTEN!

I come into contact with so many people who never listen to a damned word I'm saying. Instead, they're planning what they're going to say next. An executive I had a meeting with recently nearly drove me screaming out of the conference room. Several people gathered together to discuss a software interface issue and cast their vote on how the issue should be implemented. Here is just a snippet of the conversation I had:

DEAF EXEC
Where's Bob? Is he coming?

ME
He has a conference call with the development company. He'll be a little late, but he told me that his vote is to have the menu bar triggered by an icon in the bottom right of the screen.

DEAF EXEC
Well, that's not Bob's decision to make. He's not in a position to decide himself. This is a team vote.

ME
Yeah, I know. I just meant that Bob's vote is yes to the icon, that's all.

DEAF EXEC
You see, when the whole team is involved in the decision, everyone can claim some sense of ownership. It's not up to one person to make the decisions anymore.

ME
I know that. So does Bob. I was just telling you what his vote was.

DEAF EXEC
We're all going to vote—

ME
Sweet baby Jesus, deliver me from this madness!

It was pointless. I shut my mouth and counted down the days until my contract expired. Learn to listen, and you'll be a breath of fresh air to everyone you interact with.

2. Don't brag and tell war stories in meetings

No one wants to hear you; you're not the most interesting person in the world. No one really gives a monkey's ass about your past. They want to accomplish what needs to be accomplished in the meeting and get out. Just zip it. Please.

3. Don't cut people off and try to finish their thoughts

I'd like to disembowel every single bastard who has the nerve to interrupt me and put words in my mouth. Let people finish their thoughts, for God's sake!

4. Don't pout and become antisocial when you don't get your way

The Dungeon Troll, the most annoying employee I ever managed, always pulled this stunt. He'd get mad, turn red, look straight ahead, cross his arms, and stick out his lower lip.

5. Don't verbally masturbate by spewing psychobabble and buzzwords

May your tongue dry up and fall out of your head if you subject others to this kind of verbal torture. If you're going to talk, say something.

6. Don't open your mouth unless you know what you're going to say

Don't babble. Pause. Take your time. Formulate your thoughts. Learn to explain things *concisely*. Get to the point with as few words as possible.

7. Don't be uncertain

Be confident and act as if everything you say is God's law. The more certain and confident you are, the less you'll be second-guessed.

8. Don't take shit and don't hand it out

If you heap out abuse, expect it in return.

9. Don't be afraid of center stage

Learn to make effective presentations. Take speech classes to sharpen your skills. Practice. It's not just a business presentation, it's show biz. Put on a dog-and-pony show. Make eye contact. Call people by their names. Learn to give concise, compelling presentations laced with a bit of humor, and you'll climb the ladder much faster than your peers who stammer their way through boring Powerpoint presentations and sweat through their clothes.

91. DON'T DO THE WRITE THING WRONG

Learn how to write if you want to stay happily employed. Writing is part of almost every job, especially since E-mail has become such an integral part of interoffice communication.

If you're a poor writer, start by taking a writing class at your local college. Just make sure that you start with a basic grammar review. Don't jump into classes like "Structuring the Novel" before you know how to use a semicolon.

KISS—Keep It Simple, Stupid! There's no better writing advice. Shorter is better. Your writing should be simple, tight, and easy on the eye. There's no Pulitzer Prizes for memos and E-mails (not yet, at least), so don't write long, complex sentences with a lot of clauses.

Your sole objective is to get the thoughts that are rattling around in your mind on paper in an organized manner, using as few words as possible.

I'm not going to get into specific common writing blunders and how to correct them. There are plenty of books out there that can teach you grammar, punctuation, and sentence construction. Some of my favorites are:

The Elements of Style by William Strunk, Jr., and E. B. White (Macmillan)

Pinckert's Practical Grammar: A Lively, Unintimidating Guide to Usage, Punctuation, and Style by Robert C. Pinckert (Writer's Digest Books)

Grammatically Correct: The Writer's Guide to Punctuation, Spelling, Style, Usage, and Grammar by Anne Stilman (Writer's Digest Books)

The Elements of Grammar by Margaret Shertzer (Collier Books)

Essentials of English by Vincent F. Hopper, Cedric Gale, Ronald C. Foote, and Benjamin W. Griffith (Barron's)

The Well-Tempered Sentence: A Punctuation Handbook for the Innocent, the Eager, and the Doomed by Karen Elizabeth Gordon (Ticknor and Fields)

The Transitive Vampire: A Handbook of Grammar for the Innocent, the Eager, and the Doomed by Karen Elizabeth Gordon (Times Books)

Buy some of these books. Study them. Do the exercises. Like anything else, if you take your writing seriously and keep practicing, you'll get better. Soon you may be the Hemingway of the Friday progress report.

92. SPELLING STILL COUNTS

Carefully spell-check every sentence you write, and do it the old-fashioned way—reach for the dictionary. I love my dictionary. Next to Madonna's *Sex,* it's my favorite book. I hope they cremate me with it when I die. I've been through a lot with that book. I've referenced most of its 2000+ pages—even used it as a murder weapon when I dropped it on a trespassing scorpion in my kitchen. I never get angry or frustrated when I have to look something up, because I know I'll always learn something new.

Never rely only on computer spell-checkers to do your work for you. They're not reliable. In fact, they can wreak havoc. One of the funniest mistakes I've witnessed was made by an executive working for an entertainment powerhouse, a guy I'll call Max Brainman. Max, the walking definition of arrogance, sent a thirty-page technical memo out to more than a hundred people from several divisions via mass E-mail. Max abbreviated the word engineer—which appeared no fewer than sixty times in the report—so that it read *engr.* The spell-checker flagged *engr.* and recommended the word *Negro* as its replacement. Max must have carelessly clicked on the "Change All" option and never bothered to double-check his work before sending it out. A hundred stunned readers received the memo the next morning. Max's proposed Negro exchange program caused quite a ruckus.

Of course, Max couldn't simply admit that he screwed up. Instead, he claimed that someone had hacked into his system and sabotaged the document. Even when a technician showed him how the mistake was made, he denied doing it. To Max, it was a conspiracy right up there with the Kennedy assassination.

93. YOUR OFFICE IS A STAGE

If you can't act, you won't go far in the business world. You must differentiate between the real world and the theater that is work. Play your part. Don a costume that conceals your true self. Prepare for your role and emotionally distance yourself from your part.

When I think about corporate theater, a former coworker comes to mind. He was a great guy and a talented employee. His problem was that he couldn't hide the fact that he detested his boss. Because he couldn't mask his contempt with a big phony "team player" mask, he was driven out of the organization.

We're all required to swallow heaps of dung in the workplace, so learn to put a smile on your face while you're staring at your boss and imagining a thousand ways to end his miserable life.

Unlike real actors, though, you'll have no script to rely on. Improvisation is the key to success. One of my coworkers was called into his boss's office and handed a copy of his own résumé, which a headhunter had carelessly faxed to the company. His livid boss was prepared to banish him to the doghouse for being disloyal, but my friend, whom I'll call Dustin Pacino, seized the moment and turned the tables by delivering an Oscar-worthy soliloquy about how he felt overworked, how management made him feel unappreciated, how he felt he had no choice but to leave. His shallow boss fell for it. With his neck on the chopping block, Dustin rose to the occasion and tooted his own horn to such an extent that instead of getting in trouble, he walked away with a raise.

94. APPEARANCES ARE STILL IMPORTANT

Like it or not, appearances are critical. The way you look, the clothes you wear, the way you speak, and the manner in which you gesture are critically important to your business success. Stand up straight. Look as if you own the world, not as if you're struggling to carry it on your shoulders.

Go out and buy nice clothes. They don't need to be Hugo Boss or Armani. Just look professional and neat. And make sure your clothes fit. I'm certainly not perfect, so don't think I'm pointing fingers. I'm a big guy with a big gut, but I still wear decent clothes. I don't buy clothes that are a size too small and try to fool myself. I don't button my pants below my hips like a lot of people who think they're still the same size they were in high school. I buy clothes that are my size even though they have more Xs on the tag than a Ron Jeremy double feature.

I'm not going to recommend that you join a gym or go on a diet. That would be as hypocritical as a Keith Richards "just say no" public service announcement. You are who you are, flaws and all. But dressing well can cover a lot of those flaws.

Spending money on clothes is an investment, not an expense. Great clothes can be wonderful tools of intimidation. When you're looking sharp, you're more confident about everything. Buy clothes that flatter you. Wear good shoes. Find colors that suit you. Get a hairstyle that works. Use deodorant. I'm always shocked and chagrined when coworkers forget to honor the basic fundamentals of grooming.

One of my employees always smelled like a rotten corpse that had been left in the sun for a week. It didn't take long for the other employees to start complaining, but what the hell could I do about it—bathe him myself? I couldn't bring myself to tell someone he stunk. The issue resolved itself when an employee put a bar of Irish Spring and a tube of Speed Stick on his chair one morning. Horribly cruel, but effective.

95. GET OFF THE POT

Don't wait to be handed orders. *Take initiative and solve problems without being told to do so.* You'll immediately catapult yourself into the highest echelon of the worldwide workforce. I don't think I'm exaggerating when I say that.

So many of the people I've managed had to be told exactly what to do and how to do it day in and day out. Whenever I hired someone who demonstrated even an inkling of initiative, who found new and better ways to do things and solve problems, I felt as if I had been sent an angel from Heaven.

In the past, I've made the mistake of letting too many people off the hook by solving their problems for them. That does nothing but create a lazy workforce. Plus, you double or triple your own workload. If I had to do it over, when an employee came to me and said something like, "What should I do?" I'd try my best to muster the guts to say, "I don't know. That's your job. Figure it out."

As an employee, if you see an opportunity to improve the process in an unobtrusive way, do it. As a manager, don't be forced to micromanage just because you're too nice to let people hang. For the sake of your bottom line and future growth, encourage people to think for themselves.

96. YOU'RE NOT THE CENTER OF THE UNIVERSE

Keep your ego in check. If you poll a thousand workers and ask them what they hate most about their jobs, I'd bet money that an egotistical prick telling them how to do their work tops the list.

In business, you have to be self-confident, even a little cocky, but as soon as you cross the threshold between confidence and a fat head, you're in the soup. And if you really start believing that a bigger title and a fatter paycheck make you better than the people working for you, you're a lost soul.

I've witnessed dozens of people suffer the symptoms of Sudden Asshole Syndrome after they were promoted. They quit returning phone calls and responding to correspondence. They talk down to people. They treat their new employees like the great unwashed. It's one of the things about business that really breaks my heart. I just want to shake people when they change for the worse and shout, "What happened to the nice person I knew?"

It's a mystery to me why people sell out so easily. Could good people really be buying into all the corporate hierarchy crap? Could they really believe that because they said the right thing in the right place at the right time it makes them better, smarter, more talented? I suppose that since work plays such an important, time-consuming part in our lives, a lot of people derive their entire self-image and identity from it. Either that, or there really are aliens taking over human bodies.

Regardless, arrogance is poison. An executive I'll call Barbara Bartlett handed out a wordy document to several hundred employees that featured famous inspirational quotes, like the ones you'll find in *Bartlett's Familiar Quotations*. Quotes are fine, but Barbara had the audacity to pepper her procedural manual with several quotes from herself alongside pearls of wisdom from Einstein, Emerson, Picasso, Shaw, and Twain. Here's one of them:

The best trait possible for humans is seldom affordable and hardly ever appreciated.
—Barbara Bartlett

Good God, what does that psychobabble mean? I think my favorite was:

Creativity is the soul; Technology is the mind.
—Barbara Bartlett

Barbara just didn't know the meaning of the word *humble*. But then again, she didn't know the meaning of most words. When, like Barbara, you let arrogance blind you, you shouldn't be collecting fat paychecks and stock options, you should be cutting out paper dolls in an asylum somewhere.

If you have a giant ego, deflate it for your own good. If you're working for a megalomaniac, try not to let it get under your skin. Laugh at him; don't let him give you an ulcer.

Not to be outdone by Barbara, I think I'll end this section with my very own quote:

Ignorant, egocentric, untalented executives who believe they are gods among mortals should be hog-tied and beaten severely by the very employees they seek to subjugate.
—F. J. Lennon

97. QUIT HIDING BEHIND E-MAIL

E-mail can be great and E-mail can be awful. With the advent of E-mail, several disturbing trends have emerged. One of them is the birth of the E-mail tough guy. Isn't it amazing how many gutless wonders suddenly grow a pair when they're composing E-mail? Alone, locked away in the solitude of their offices, these E-mail rogues type venomous messages dripping with sarcastic criticism, but confront them face to face, and they don't have the guts to look you in the eye. *If you're a ballbreaker via E-mail, have the guts to also be one live and in person.*

Another disturbing trend is using E-mail to cover tracks and pass the blame. Employees spend too much time crafting carefully worded E-mails and sifting through bogus E-mails instead of working. Here's a scenario I see all the time: an employee screws up, but instead of taking the blame, he spends three hours composing a craftily worded E-mail that shifts the blame to someone else. Then he sends his message to the entire company. The employee now being blamed has to retaliate. She spends the next day writing her defense, again shifting the blame and blind-copying it to everyone. Before you know it, everyone is wasting valuable hours of the day sifting through E-mail chains while trying to get to the bottom of who really dropped the ball. Because of E-mail, too many tiny troubles are suddenly magnified into life-and-death crises.

Use E-mail sensibly.

98. YOU'RE NOT MADONNA

For God's sake, choose a self and stand by it.
—William James

As long as you work at a company, maintain the image you've created for yourself. *Don't change your identity in midstream.* It doesn't work. Just be who you are and quit trying to be the flavor of the week.

A major executive at an entertainment company I worked for—a man I'll call Rudolph Hefner—created a corporate image (at least in his own mind) in which he was a supercharged alpha male always on the prowl for sex. I've seen business associates create phony images in honor of business giants, politicians, and movie characters, but this particular pimp personality was unique. What made watching Rudy in action even more nauseating was that he was an ugly little twerp who, without his six-figure salary and Porsche, couldn't get a date on this or any other world. Rudy's machismo didn't earn him the love and respect of his female coworkers; it earned him a warning for sexual harassment.

One putz I worked with changed his identity more often than Dennis Rodman changes the color of his hair. We always had an informal dress code at work. It was pretty much jeans and sneakers every day, unless there was going to be an important meeting with outsiders. The Monday after this guy saw *Pretty Woman*, he came into the office wearing a Richard Gere–style suit and hairstyle. The fancy duds and Hollywood coiffure lasted for about two weeks, which was the norm for one of his many incarnations. For brief periods, he became Gordon Gekko from *Wall Street*, Viper from *Top Gun*, Bill Gates (complete with spectacles, sharp tongue, and disorganized, wrinkled look), and Tony Robbins (with motivational posters for the office walls). This guy was really depriving a village somewhere of a great idiot.

99. DON'T BE A TRAVELING TERROR

When your job requires you to travel, behave yourself. What you say and do in public is a reflection of your business, and with the countless temptations facing corporate travelers, it's easy to get into trouble.

Especially in my twenties, business travel was an excuse to party. Drinking to excess was clearly part of my skill set.

One of my former coworkers was a traveling terror. During the biggest industry trade show of the year, we suddenly fell short of promotional items like caps and T-shirts at our booth because he had given them to the two prostitutes he had subcontracted for an evening's employment. I'm still waiting for the day I turn on *Cops* and see hookers clad in my old company's T-shirts being dragged out of a bordello.

It's a mystery, but it's also a fact—people use business travel as an excuse to lead double lives. When they're away from home in a strange city where no one knows them, they are tempted to, as Jung would say, embrace their shadow selves. Some people on business trips conduct adulterous affairs, visit strip clubs and peep shows, and solicit hookers. Sometimes they get caught, lose their jobs, and even ruin their lives.

Last year, two major executives in the dot-com world were charged for propositioning minors over the Internet. One of the executives even made a trip to meet the young girl he was soliciting. When he arrived he fell into an FBI sting and was arrested. Child pornography was discovered on his laptop. His career was over before the age of forty.

My all-time favorite "traveling terror" story is about a major investment banking executive who, in 1995, went on a hellish drinking binge before boarding a twelve-hour flight from Argentina to New York. The president of Portugal and other government representatives, on their way to the United Nations' fiftieth anniversary celebration, shared the first-class cabin with this executive. When flight attendants refused to serve him any more alcohol, he went ballistic. He told a flight attendant that he would "bust his ass" and then shoved another attendant into a seat. The rampage reached its zenith when the executive climbed on top of a service cart, tore off his pants, and proceeded to evacuate his bowels.

The formal complaint says that "[the executive] then used linen napkins as toilet paper and wiped his hands on various service counters and service implements used by the crew and then tracked feces throughout the aircraft."

I'm glad I wasn't flying the friendly skies with him. He not only embraced his shadow self, he damn near copulated with it.

100. YOU CAN MAKE IT ANYWHERE

For years, I worked in the small town where I grew up. My company was based there, and I never gave much thought to leaving until I was forced to. My small-town upbringing sank deep into my marrow. There were countless times during my years in business when I gave serious thought to walking away from my company and venturing out to work for one of the giants in my industry. Somehow, though, those fantasies seemed implausible, even though I was good at my job.

It has been years since I left, and I can now see how small-minded I was. My wife was the same way. Long before we were married, I would tell her that she had a true knack for designing children's software and should be doing it for one of the biggies, but she scoffed at the notion as if it were an impossible dream.

Ours were far from being from impossible dreams. My wife is doing exactly what I used to her encourage her to do, and I've overcome the professional doubts that used to prevent me from approaching industry giants. We should have realized that because we were good at our jobs, we were good enough to work for any company, anywhere.

Don't doubt yourself. There's no rule that says that just because you work for a small company in a small town, you can't work for one of your industry's heavyweights.

101. QUIT BITCHING: LIFE ISN'T FAIR

Do not expect justice where might is right.
—Phaedrus

Are there rules for success? Perhaps a few basic fundamentals, but certainly no rules. Hard work isn't enough. Neither is talent. Is it luck? Fate? Who knows? But there are a lot of untalented, obnoxious, piss-poor human beings making too much money and wielding too much power in today's corporate culture.

It's clear to me that *sometimes bad people win and nice people lose.* This problem has been around since the really brave and skilled hunters had to give the best hunks of woolly mammoth meat to the lazy, generally stupid, but powerful apeman in charge back at the cave. A million years from now, it'll be the same story. Injustice is just part of human nature. The fact that there's so much unfairness in the workplace really used to get to me. I'll be honest, it still sometimes does. But take it from me—don't try to figure out why or wait around for justice to be served, or you'll drive yourself mad.

Don't cry foul. Business, like life, is anything but fair. If it were fair, most of the bosses I've worked for would be asking me if I wanted to Supersize my Value Meal.

Several less-than-stellar people who have worked for me and with me are multimillionaires, at least on paper. There's really no rhyme or reason why some of them hit the jackpot and others didn't. Most of them were in the right place at the right time. One of these people was a computer programmer from Russia whom I'll call Ivan Bigbuckski. Ivan desperately wanted to flee his job at the Russian National Academy of Science and relocate his family to either Britain or the United States. He designed some addictive and challenging arcade games, along the lines of the megahit *Tetris.* Ivan hoped that his puzzle games were his ticket out of Russia. He couldn't find a publisher in Europe, so he employed the services of an agent who was my friend. She showed me the games, and I loved them. Ivan got a visa and came to America to complete his work; it was his first trip to the States. He was hoping to see the Statue of Liberty, but New York my small suburban town wasn't. I put Ivan up in a modest hotel, but you would have thought that I had booked him a suite at the Ritz. After dinner the first night, I asked him what he wanted to do next, maybe a drink or a movie. No. Ivan wanted to visit the local supermarket. When he walked into the Giant Eagle, he had a look on his face as if he were gazing at the Sistine Chapel. For over an hour, he walked every aisle and studied the price tags; he nearly wet himself with joy because you could buy veal, chicken, beef, and pork at the same time!

Ivan stayed for more than a month. He was a decent, funny man and a hard worker. Unfortunately, his games didn't sell well. He did, however, earn just enough in royalties to take up residence in London, where his agent dug up some additional contract work for him so that he could start saving to pay for his family's relocation. Less than two years later, Ivan hit the jackpot. He ended up licensing a few of his puzzle games to Microsoft, who wanted to include them in something they were calling "Windows." A year after that, he was converting classic arcade games like Pac-Man and Asteroids to the PC for *Microsoft's Windows Arcade Pack*, and getting paid royalties for every unit shipped!

Ivan became a multimillionaire while I was still clipping coupons from the same Giant Eagle where we walked the aisles together. The last I heard, he was living the good life in London.

The year that stress nearly got the best of me was 1995. Here's a quick recap: In February, my sister died. Three weeks later, my dad died. In May, I got married. In July, my company sent me off-site to work on a project for a month. In August, my boss started sticking it to me in an attempt to get me to quit so that that the company didn't have to pay out my contract. From August until my contract expired, I stayed in a work environment I hated. Then, to top the year of years off, I said farewell to my family and friends, sold my house, and relocated to Los Angeles, a place where I swore I'd never live in a million years, a place that didn't even have a professional football team!

Was it fair that my life got turned upside down? I hope not, or else I must have been a dentist in my past life. I made the mistake of expecting that justice would be served and the people who screwed me would get their comeuppance. But it never really happened. I asked, "Why me?" about a million times, but when no definitive answers came from the clouds or from my own inner voice, life rolled on. Things got better. In fact, things were soon better than ever. There's a Chinese proverb that says, *"Every character must be chewed to get to its juice."* Well, I got chewed good and hard that year, but I survived. If I can make it through a year like that, I now know I can make it through anything. Maybe it takes being pushed to the brink to find out who you really are.

There are times when work just plain sucks. There are days when I'd rather be sick than be at work. There are times when I feel so trapped that I see bars on my office door and windows; work feels like a hopeless prison of measured time. But then there are days when I actually find my job thrilling.

The longer you hang in there, the better your odds are for success. Business is a marathon, not a sprint. Don't give up. Work always has its seasons and waves. In spring, you might be on the blacklist, but by Christmas, you could be the savior, the golden child of the office.

On Ronald Reagan's final morning as president, he rose early and went to the Oval Office. Alone at his desk, Reagan penned a personal note to his successor, George Bush, on his little pad of paper with letterhead that read: DON'T LET THE TURKEYS GET YOU DOWN. Reagan began the note by saying:

Dear George,
You'll have moments when you want to use this particular stationary. Well, go for it.

It's good advice for a President of the United States and for the rest of us.

102. DON'T GET BOGGED DOWN IN THE MUCK

Don't let problems make you unproductive. I'm guilty of crawling into my shell when times got tough. If I could do it over, I would make an extra effort to keep plugging away during my company's darkest days.

Weeks would go by when I would sit at my desk, do little or no work, worry, and obsess about every negative possibility. I would paint worst-case scenarios in my mind; negativity and fear were my watercolors.

By noon each day, I would start the countdown to the only hour I cared about—happy hour. During my worst business crisis, I hung a dartboard in my office to take my mind off of my business woes. Darts became an obsession. While the phone rang off the hook with angry creditors calling for their money and the stack of bills grew taller, I was tossing darts like a world champion on a British pub tour.

The Year of the Bull's-Eye, as it came to be known, was only one of many episodes when I let negativity and doubt swallow me whole, when I allowed depression to stifle my ability to work. In the end, I always snapped out of my funk just before it was too late. Believe me, worrying did no good.

Try to get perspective. I know it's easy to say and really hard to do, but keep at it. Work is not worth suffering over. Illness is. So is losing your loved ones. But business? No way.

The founder of the college I attended was a Benedictine monk who came to America from Germany in 1846. I've read a lot about

Abbot Boniface Wimmer and his many struggles in establishing a monastery and a college in a foreign land. He always repeated a phrase that became his epitaph:

> *Our customary tendency to move forward must continue.*
> *Forward, always forward, everywhere forward. We cannot be held*
> *back by debts, by the difficulties of the times, by unfortunate years.*
> *Man's adversity is God's opportunity.*

Take Wimmer's wise advice. *Move forward when adversity sets in.*

103. IT'S STILL ONLY YOUR JOB, FOR GOD'S SAKE

Don't let work become the only thing in your life. I made this mistake when I was in my twenties, and I now wish I could reclaim much of the time I wasted holed up in my office around the clock. You're only young once. I should have been more active and carefree. I should have played more golf. Instead, I defined myself by my work. I and my business were one. I carried it with me always, and I sacrificed much of my precious youth.

Now I try to get a grip. Think about it—in fifty or sixty years, we'll all be dead. Most of our work will be forgotten. The accomplishments for which we're sacrificing our personal lives will be monuments of archaic technology in just a few years.

Of the forty published software products that I've worked on, only a handful are still in the marketplace. That's because I'm in a technology-driven industry in which products released five years ago look ancient today. Only a decade ago, I sweated blood and pulled all-nighters for computer games that I can't even play now because the 5¼" disk drive is obsolete. People who aren't even born yet may dig through digital archives and find something I've left behind, but chances are, these same people will look at my offerings and chuckle, the same way we laugh at old eight-track tape players. Maybe a few of our accomplishments may truly outlive us if we're lucky, but not many.

When it's all said and done, do you think you'll be kicking yourself on Judgment Day for not putting in more time at the office? It's the times when you put your job over your family and friends, the weekends you sacrificed, the vacations you cancelled because of work that will haunt you.

My late father worked at one company for thirty-six years. When he started, it was a small family organization, but it grew to become a global corporation. He worked tirelessly to help put that company on the map, but by the end of his career, he was pushed aside like so many older executives in his position. It hurt. When he retired, they gave him a gold watch, but he never wore it. When he died, not a single representative of that company visited the funeral home or even sent flowers. A few months after his death, I got the watch refurbished, and I wear it every day. I wear it to remind me of my dad, but mostly, I wear it to remind myself not to take my career so seriously.

A job is a job, plain and simple. There are many others like it. It's not what matters most. I urge you to have a life outside of work and put some emotional distance between you and your projects. Be proud of the work you do, but be realistic. *What you're making yourself sick over today will mean nothing in a few years.*

And don't go jumping off a bridge if your company goes under or you get fired. "This too shall pass." As impossible as that sometimes seems, it's true. I've made the epic mistake of allowing work stress to manifest a wide array of physical ailments and take years off my life. Business is not about life and death, so get a grip. Learn to embrace the worst-case scenario. If you get fired, you struggle for a few months, and then you get a new job. If your company goes under, you deal with a lot of legal and personal crap for a year or two, and then you move on.

EPILOGUE

To Forgive, Divine

The biggest mistake people make in life is
not trying to make a living
at doing what they most enjoy.
—Malcolm Forbes

A failure is a man who has blundered,
but is not able to cash in on the experience.
—Elbert Hubbard

Well, that's it—every mistake in my book. There are probably a few hundred other smaller business mistakes I could write about, but those are the major ones.

I feel as if I've just left the confessional. What do you think? Should I be forgiven for my business sins? I hope so. I'll bet you've made a few of them yourself, or work closely with someone who has.

Screwing up and watching those around us do the same is how we learn. History's greatest lessons were born from epic mistakes. The sad part is not the mistakes themselves, but the fact that history always seems to repeat itself. The successful people in business and in life are the ones who learn from their mistakes, profit from them, and stop repeating them.

During the last holiday season, my wife and I went to Disneyland to soak up the dazzling lights and Christmas decorations. There was an unusually small crowd that night, so the ride lines were short. We kept riding the old nostalgic rides in Fantasyland over and over— Snow White's Adventures, Pinocchio, Mr. Toad's Wild Ride, Peter Pan's Flight—and I became aware of something that applies to this book. Most of these rides have a common theme. At some point, someone sensible advises, "Don't do it" or "Don't go there," or a road sign warns "Danger ahead!" But what did Pinocchio do? What did Mr. Toad do? They ignored the warnings that were smack dab in front of them and made a big mistake. But the adventure only really began after the big blunder was committed. And in the end, all turned out well as long as they all had good hearts.

As I bring my tale to a close, I feel oddly torn. I look back on the early days of my career, and it feels like an old dream that never really happened. Part of me is proud of what I've accomplished; the other part feels as if my brain must have been shut off for at least half my career.

I also feel torn when I think about the amazing cast of characters I've had the pleasure and misfortune of working with. If they were all assembled before me now, I'd smile warmly at some of them for their friendship and humor. I'd try to hide from others. I'd look for a large metal object to beat several of them with. I'd nod with respect and gratitude to those who inspired me. I'd laugh at all of the tyrants for their magnificent arrogance, stupidity, and insecurity, and say a silent prayer for all those who have to tolerate them (because they're still out there). And I'd probably buy each and every one of them a drink because at one time or another, we were all in the same boat together.

I hope that a few of the topics I've written about will remain with you. If I can prevent you from making some of the same mistakes I made, then I've done my job. I also hope you had a laugh or two.

My final bit of advice is straightforward: Be cool, work hard, play nice, use your noggin, exercise common sense, don't burn bridges, and don't be a snake.

Thank you for reading. Good luck and good business to you.

Acknowledgments

There are a number of people I'd like to thank:

First, my mother, Jean Lennon, the most honorable role model of my life. Thank you for your love, support, friendship—and for the million things you've done for me.

My wonderful (and extensive) family and my many friends for your continued encouragement and friendship. If I thanked you all by name, the list would be as long this book. So to each of you, I say thanks. And now that I've thanked you, you all have to buy at least one copy of this book.

All of my coworkers, past and present, friend and foe. We've all learned many valuable lessons together.

Jonathon and Wendy Lazear, Christi Cardenas, Tanya Cromey, Laura Brinkmeier, and everyone at the Lazear Agency for their continued encouragement and representation over the last five years.

Laura Yorke for taking on this project.

Cal Morgan and Cassie Jones for their excellent editorial assistance. And Jamilet Ortiz and everyone else at ReganBooks.

Dr. William Snyder for teaching me a great deal about writing when I attended St. Vincent College.

And finally, my wife, Laura, the best manager I know, for your assistance in shaping this book and for your unconditional support while I took a leap of faith.